THE ORIGINS AND DEVELOPMENT OF AFRICAN THEOLOGY

THE ORIGINS AND DEVELOPMENT OF AFRICAN THEOLOGY

Gwinyai H. Muzorewa

ORBIS BOOKS

Maryknoll, New York 10545

The Catholic Foreign Mission Society of America (Maryknoll) recruits and trains people for overseas missionary service. Through Orbis Books Maryknoll aims to foster the international dialogue that is essential to mission. The books published, however, reflect the opinions of their authors and are not meant to represent the official position of the society.

Manuscript Editor: Mary Heffron

Library of Congress Cataloging in Publication Data

Muzorewa, Gwinyai H.
  The origins and development of African theology.

  Bibliography: P.
  Includes index.
  1. Theology, Doctrinal—Africa, Sub-Saharan—History—20th century.
2. Black theology.   I. Title.
BT30.A438M88   1985   230'.096   84-14769
ISBN 0-88344-351-1 (pbk.)

Contents

Preface

As an ordained African minister serving the United Methodist Church, one of the major denominations founded and sponsored by missionaries, I am very concerned about the origin, development, content, and future of African theology.

I was born and raised in a United Methodist family. My parents believe that God comes first in whatever we do. They insist on prayers before meals and before going to sleep. They also believe that one begins one's day with prayers. Very often, during the evening devotions when I was a child, either my mother or father or both would break into tears. This frightened me because I could never understand how they got to that degree of what I may characterize as emotional intensity. But no one commented or asked any questions. In general, family devotions ended on a very sad note.

When I was a little older, I realized that my mother had a chronic disease, but neither Western doctors nor African traditional doctors were able to help her. My parents visited all sorts of African medical experts as well as African spirit healers—all in vain. Neither did ceaseless prayers make any observable difference.

I was old enough to remember when they visited Mai Chaza, referred to by some as "Mother Savior."* Whenever there was a religious revival, my parents were sure to attend and actively participate. The religious theme that was emphasized the most was the belief that there is no name greater than Jesus. Only he could carry our burdens if we turned to him.

However, our American missionary pastors and their indigenous assistants did not approve of emotional behavior. A certain "Christian"

---

*She was said to have risen from the dead and to have spiritual powers to heal the sick and enable the barren to conceive. However, even she did not succeed in healing mother. Mai Chaza has established an independent church called *Guta ra Jehova*, meaning "the city of God," with its headquarters in Zimunya Reserve.

decorum was expected and even enforced, not only at the revivals but in the regular Sunday worship service. I can still hear some of our Western-trained African pastors saying *ngatizvibatenyi*, "let us behave ourselves." These clergymen suppressed free African expression and instilled a Western form of dignity. The artificial atmosphere enforced by missionaries seriously stifled the African spiritually.

Years later, I became a licensed preacher, even though I had only a basic knowledge of the catechism and the Scriptures. I ran into more difficult religious situations. I was also old enough to raise questions in my own heart. I began to wonder why God had not answered my parents' ceaseless prayers.

Worse still, although my father was a local preacher and my mother was a prominent member of the *Rukwadzano* Society (United Methodist Women), tragedy hit us just like any other family. I remember the tragic death of my sister's first child who was living with us. He was only two and one-half years old when he died. He never really fell sick.

I remember my parents questioning why God had permitted this to happen. They concluded that the devil was tempting them. In fact this tragic death had a lot more implications. My parents had lost their first child too. So they asked: Why our first grandchild as well? Is this some kind of fate?

In spite of this suffering, meaningless as far as we were concerned, my parents and the rest of the family continued to believe that God is almighty, all-powerful, all-knowing, and omnipresent. We all maintained the belief that the name of Jesus still had the power to deliver us from evil. All this influenced my faith.

To the best of my recollection, I did not join other churches for no reason except that my parents were United Methodists, then known as the American Methodists. I was not aware of any theological or confessional differences between our church and other denominations.

In the late fifties, throughout the sixties, and culminating in the seventies, I became aware of another dimension to many problems. The political struggle between the white oppressors and the black people in what is now Zimbabwe heightened and intensified.

Our church was then run by predominantly white missionaries who gave us the impression that anything Western and white was noble and Christian. It was certainly superior to anything African. For instance, the Western style of housing was always considered better than the African traditional style. We were taught that a piano was more conducive to worship than the African drums. An African child with an English name was considered Christian while one with an African name was regarded as pagan. This is why I was named Henry at baptism rather than Gwinyai.

White people inside and outside the church seemed to have the same attitude toward the Africans. They naturally occupied all the high positions. For example, in the United Methodist Church, the bishop and most of the district superintendents were white missionaries. Although in my country the ratio between blacks and whites was twenty to one, we, the black folks, seemed to be the strangers, especially in the urban areas. The official language in the private sector, as well as the government circles, was English. An African who could speak good English was more respected than one who could not.

It was during this time (1957) that a wind of change blew from Ghana, hitherto known as the Gold Coast. The political pronouncements from people like Kwame Nkrumah, one of the major exponents of Pan-Africanism and African nationalism, transformed numerous Africans who had fallen prey to white imperialism.

It was the spirit of African nationalism and Pan-Africanism that opened my eyes to the apparent contradictions between the gospel of Jesus Christ as it was proclaimed in the mission churches and the African social reality as I experienced it. At times it appeared as if the politicians spoke to my needs more than the preachers did.

Because theology is one of the very few disciplines that attempts to deal with African life holistically, I have developed tremendous and lifetime interests in it. What does it have to say to, and about, the African who finds himself or herself in a situation where the very agency of the gospel of Jesus Christ turns out to be inseparable from the agency of oppression, racism, and dehumanization? How can the same agency preach meaningfully about love, humanity, liberation, and human dignity? This concern is what prompts my interest in theology.

Maybe an African interpretation of the Scriptures could be more meaningful and relevant to the Africans. Consequently, I think that a discussion on a new African hermeneutic could possibly uncover the true message of Jesus Christ for the sick, the poor, and the oppressed people in Africa. I contend that African theology, as a reflection on the praxis of the African's survival strategy, interpreted in the light of God's grace and justice which is revealed in the Scriptures, can answer many crucial survival questions among the African people. Consequently, my interest in African theology is due to my personal, as well as our collective, concern for the survival of the black people in the continent and in diaspora. Thus it warrants a thorough study.

Acknowledgments

Many persons were involved in the inception and development of this study. It is not possible to mention them all. Bishop J. Yeakle and his cabinet, the Oswego Center, and Southwest Oswego United Methodist Churches in New York facilitated my doctoral studies by employing me as their part-time pastor, with the understanding that I was, first and foremost, a doctoral student. While their "pastor" was commuting between Syracuse and New York City, they literally took care of my family (especially during the upstate blizzards!). I appreciate also the help of Bishop Monk Bryan and Rev. Dick Carter and the United Methodist congregations I served for a brief period in Crawford and Whitney, Nebraska.

Words cannot express the extent of my gratitude to Union Theological Seminary. President Donald Shriver is the friendliest and most resourceful administrator I have ever known. Dean Robert Handy was not only dean but pastor, because he used pastoral approaches to help me deal with my academic concerns. My deepest gratitude to Dr. John H. Hendrickson whose decision to award me the Masland Fellowship brought about significant and positive changes in my life.

Professor Roger Shinn, in his capacity as academic advisor, gave me the most effective tools with which to fight my academic battles. He is a man who practices what he teaches and has great respect for cultures. Professor Christopher Morse's method of teaching and conducting seminars in systematic theology inspired me to pursue systematics, culminating in my interest in third world theologies and a focus on African theology.

Without Professor James H. Cone's academic excellence, and his influence even in Africa, I would not have applied to Union in the first place and the present study would not have been possible. Professor Cone gave me what the United States as such could not: the pride and confidence that black people can join hands together, both at work and leisure. In his humility, Professor Cone has skillfully imparted to me the sense of a theological author. I thank him for his untiring commitment to help me through my investigations to a happy end. I thank both Professor Gayraud Wilmore and Professor Cone for giving me access to their personal libraries, in addition to personal and professional advice.

Were it not for my two good friends, Rev. Christopher Jokomo and Mr. David Danga, who assisted me financially, it would have taken forever to do this study. My father, Haadi, and mother, Takaruda, volunteered much useful information long before I started my research.

My wife, Sue, was my first audience in the developing and testing of my ideas. She encouraged me, without ceasing, to persevere when both the spirit and the body were discouraged. In the same breath I thank my children for their "inadvertent" cooperation during the past half-decade of study.

My special thanks go to Virginia Clifford and Mary Heffron, whose editing gave this document the quality I wanted, and to Mrs. Sevcan Sevim for her professional typing.

Finally, I thank God who gave me the community that helped me become a useful vessel. Into God's hands I commend this work on African theology.

Introduction

PURPOSE

The purpose of this study is to tell the story of African theology and to analyze its origin and development. I am not aware of any other work that gives a panorama of theological reflections by Africans on the Christian faith. There are only fragments. My intention here is to state what prominent African theologians and scholars have said about the major trends of African theology.

Since there is more said than written on African theology, I do not expect to cover all that has ever been said or even written about the subject. However, I believe that works I use here will be fairly representative. I will examine several books and many pertinent articles published on African theology. It is disappointing to find that not all that carries the banner of "African Theology" is African theology at all. It is hoped that this work does not add to the shelves of these misleading works.

Furthermore, there are some articles and books that state the ideals of African theology but do not state what it actually is. I believe that I will make a contribution to theology and to the church if I am able to discriminate between the theological ideals and reality. I believe that a serious student of African theology would want to know what it is before he or she attempts to amend, supplement, or criticize it.

Therefore, the purpose of this study is to describe what African theology is: its origin, definition, sources, types, and history of development. This task needs to be done because the church in Africa south of the Sahara is concerned about its self-identity in the postcolonial era.

The missionary-sending agencies overseas are keen to hear the story of what has happened to the African church since their departure from the continent. The African nationalists want to know the thinking of the church on certain political issues. Only a statement on African theology can present a representative picture of these concerns.

John S. Mbiti has said that "the Church in Africa is a Church without a theology and a Church without theological concern" (1972c, 51). It is important that a work of this nature be written in an attempt to assess the extent of the accuracy of Mbiti's claim. If we can determine what African theology has been, what it presently is, then we will be in a position to direct its future development. Unless African theology can be stated in a coherent fashion, then it will be difficult to know what African theology has been and what it is.

However, whatever else we may say about African theology, we cannot for a moment forget to acknowledge our theological heritage even though it is limited. It has accrued over the two decades since the term *African theology* came into theological vogue in the mid-fifties and early sixties.

Most of our theologians may be classified as first generation theologians. Many African theologians were trained overseas during a time when African theology was not on the map. This phenomenon has two sides to it. On the one hand, the theological perspectives of such theologians were broadened. On the other hand, they were not prepared to do what would be most profitable to the church in Africa, namely, produce an indigenous theology. They are now confronted with the problem of doing African theology using Western theological and philosophical thought-forms.

Theological concepts have remained in foreign shells for the African people because in most of our universities and theological colleges professors and tutors tend to feel more comfortable rehashing what was said by Karl Barth and other Euro-Americans than coming to theological insights from our African social context and our reading of the Bible.

Edward W. Fashole-Luke has already mentioned the problem we are facing in African institutions.

Others continue to mouth the theological platitudes they have picked up in universities, theological seminaries or colleges abroad or parade their erudition by quoting the latest theological ideas in Europe and North America [1975, 260].

However, this is not to despise but merely to describe the African theological status quo. In fact, we have a theological heritage that lays the foundation for any future African theology.

LIMITATIONS AND BOUNDARIES

In this work my understanding of boundaries is that any materials that enhance our central concern are within the limit, and any that are irrelevant are out. However, it is still necessary to state nominal dates so that I cross over the boundaries consciously and only for a sufficient reason.

On the one hand, any talk about African theology must begin in the middle of 1950s when Fueter first used the term (1956). On the other hand, any discussion about African nationalism and Pan-Africanism must begin with people like W. E. B. DuBois in North America in the early twentieth century. This flexibility is necessary because we are examining the origins of African theology. The subject matter determines the boundaries and not vice versa.

In terms of materials we cannot confine ourselves, for instance, to South Africa when discussing the origin of black theology. We must also stretch ourselves to North America where black theology first started.

Furthermore, written materials on the subject are very scarce because much of African theology is done orally. Consequently, language presents a serious handicap. I can utilize only those materials in French, English, and Shona. The latter is my native African language.

Although I carried out thorough research on African traditional religions, I could cover only a limited region. I do not include Muslim or North African theologies or traditions. For the material on Africa south of the Sahara, I had to depend on work already done by other African scholars, such as Professor John S. Mbiti. Throughout the study I deal more with specifically Protestant theological traditions and general Christian traditions than with the Catholic tradition.

Another obvious limitation in this study, which I was aware of when I began work on it, was the fact that I am writing in the United States of America and not in Africa.

FORMAT

The two-part structure of this work develops chronologically. Part I consists of five chapters dealing with the origins or sources of African theology. Chapter 1, which discusses African traditional religion as a source of African theology, is distinct from the other four chapters in that it does not reflect the influence of the Scriptures; it depends solely on general revelation. Chapter 4, on nationalism, may seem a rather peculiar source of African theology, but the reader should appreciate that Christianity and politics are not exclusive in African theology. Chapters 2, 3, and 5, dealing with the coming of Christianity to Africa, the African independent church movement, and the All Africa Conference of Churches, respectively, belong roughly in the same category, though each warrants separate treatment.

There may be other sources of African theology besides those I treat here. I believe, however, that these five are the most important and basic ones. The order in which I discuss these sources does not necessarily signify their sequence of importance. I have chosen this particular order because it suits the format of the study.

Part II scrutinizes three major types of theology found in sub-Saharan Africa. The three types are the theology of traditional religion, African theology, and black theology in South Africa. The theology of traditional religion, treated in chapter 6, does not draw upon the Scriptures, a primary source used by all other Third World theologies; its insights come from general revelation. Although African and black theologies use a common biblical source, the former emphasizes indigenization of the faith, while the latter focuses on a particular interpretation: liberation.

PART I

SOURCES OF AFRICAN THEOLOGY

Chapter 1

African Traditional Religion

Most African theologians who are involved in the development of an African theology find that African traditional religion is one of their chief sources. In fact, their recent interest in African theology has led them to a simultaneous study of the traditional religions of their continent.

In this chapter I will discuss four ingredients of traditional religion that have provided African theologians with a skeleton for an African theology. These components are God, ancestral spirits, the concept of good and evil, and humanity.

The importance of these concepts for the origin and development of African theology is evidenced by the recent works of E. Bolaji Idowu, John S. Mbiti, and Harry Sawyerr.[1] These African scholars have turned to traditional religions for the sole purpose of ascertaining what their heritage has to offer to modern Africans who would develop an African theology. The concern of these scholars is best summed up by Harry Sawyerr's comment: "There is a strong case for a 'Theologia Africana' which will seek to interpret Christ to the African in such a way that he feels at home in the new faith" (1971b, 24).

It is out of the concern to make the African feel "at home" while being in the Christian church that Idowu wrote *Toward an Indigenous Church*. To be "at home" is, for the African, to experience continuity between traditional life and the Christian faith. A reconciliation between Christianity and African traditional religion can occur only after a careful examination of the central elements of the latter has been carried out. In *Olodumare: God in Yoruba Belief* and later in *African Traditional Religion*, Idowu has examined some of these major themes. While his book on the indigenous church calls for the indigenization of the Nigerian Methodist Church, his *Olodumare* and *African Traditional Religion* treat the subject more widely, a necessity if the African church and its theology are going to be Africanized.

Harry Sawyerr's *Creative Evangelism* and his *God: Ancestor or Creator* indicate the importance of traditional religion for the development of African theology. Of *Creative Evangelism*, Mbiti writes: "Sawyerr searches for theological understanding of Christian truths viewed from an African background" (1972b, 187).

Mbiti's work has made an enormous impact on the studies of Africa's theologians.[2] In *African Religions and Philosophy* he has made an extensive survey of the religions of the African people, while *Concepts of God in Africa* focuses on traditional concepts of the deity. *New Testament Eschatology* is Mbiti's attempt to compare Christianity with African traditional religion, emphasizing the concept of eschatology. Although the study is largely limited to the Akamba of Kenya, the author's generalizations apply to many other African peoples.

Speaking on behalf of himself and his fellow African theologians, Mbiti said:

> Our written knowledge of traditional religions is comparatively little, though increasing, and comes chiefly from anthropologists and sociologists. Practically nothing has been produced by theologians, describing or interpreting these religions theologically [1970a, 1].

This concern for African theology is reflected also in Idowu and Sawyerr's works. Thus Idowu speaks for many when he says that Africans must produce an indigenous theology. Many African theologians are, in fact, advocating a theology that develops largely out of certain major aspects of African traditional religions. As Mbiti puts it, there is "a serious attempt to see Christianity accommodated in the traditional African framework of religion and thought" (1972b, 187).

If most African theologians who are interested in the construction of an African theology believe that African traditional religion is an indispensable source, what, then, are the chief elements in this religion and why is it important?

THE CONCEPT OF GOD

All African theologians understand that the idea of God, the most important component in African traditional religion, will exert a primary influence on African theology. Most of them agree that all African peoples believe in one God. For instance, Gabriel M. Setiloane states that to note this attribute among Sotho-Tswana peoples is to state the obvious (1976b, 79). Other theologians have emphasized the fact that Africans have always believed in the one God. Moreover, Idowu says: "There is no place, age, or generation which did not receive at some point in its history some form of revelation" (1975, 140). Thus in developing a doctine of God, African theology can base its theological tenets on the one God whose self-revelation has occurred in different forms to various races and generations.

Idowu finds that although God is one, various communities may have different names for God. The many names of God, therefore, need not imply polytheistic practices in African religion; it is the same God whose self-revelation occurs throughout the world. My interpretation is supported by Malcolm J. McVeigh who says that

the God of African traditional religion and Christianity is in fact the same. God who revealed himself fully in Jesus Christ is none other than the one who has continually made himself known to African religious experience [1974a, 81].

The revelation to which both Idowu and McVeigh refer is one of the bases on which African traditionalists claim to know God. African theologians are thus developing a doctrine of God that enriches the present Christian understanding of God in Africa. Setiloane says that:

The Sotho-Tswana God, according to me, the Ngo peoples' God, according to Gaba, and the Kikuyu peoples' God, according to Kibicho, could never die, because *It* has no human limitations and *It* is so immense, incomprehensible, wide, tremendous, and unique [1979].[3]

This assertion not only reinforces the African belief that there is only one God, but also demonstrates that the categories of male and female do not apply to God.

The African belief in the one God whose self-revelation is continuous leads us to the concept of natural theology.[4] The use of both general and special revelation enables African theologians, as Harry Sawyerr has remarked, to present God as both immanent and transcendent (1963), a concept that underscores the importance of traditional religion in the formulation of an African theology.

One of the most important tasks of African theology is to be able to articulate God's relationship to humanity. In this regard the traditional belief that God is both transcendent and immanent (1970a, 41) provides a framework for understanding how the African views God. African theology needs to develop this concept in such a way that the African experience of God's presence and seeming "absence" affirm God's omnipresence. Gabriel Setiloane maintains that "God is everywhere, involved in everything . . . although *It* is in some way located in the sky and in the bowels of the earth . . . yet *It* controls everything" (1976b, 82).

My understanding of the theologian's task is to interpret concepts of God in such a way that African believers feel a natural closeness to the one God, the only Supreme Being known in African traditional religion. As Fashole-Luke says,

> In essence the nature of the quest for African Christian theologies is to translate the one faith of Jesus Christ to suit the tongue, style, genius, character and culture of the African peoples [1975, 263].

Theologians share the view that God is the *Original Source* and the *Beginning* of all things (1970, 21). In Idowu's words, "Only Deity is the absolute origin of all things, only he has absolute power and authority" (1975, 160). Mbiti has said: "Strictly speaking, Theo-Logy has to do primarily with God, and all other things must spring from that" (1972b, 186). With this background, African scholars have a solid base on which to construct a sound theology which is scriptural.[5]

Justice is another attribute of God that is important for an African theology. Setiloane declares that God preserves justice (1976b, 83). Other African theologians recognize that there is a point beyond which human and spiritual powers cannot go and only God will remain ultimately responsible. In traditional life, God is believed to intervene on certain occasions for the purpose of preserving justice. In its search for principles of justice, an African theology will draw from African traditional legal procedures. Thus it is important for African scholars to establish a theological concept of justice such that when they address political matters their theological decisions may be grounded in genuinely African tenets, and not based on Western rules.

Africans believe that while God is invisible, God's acts are tangible. Herein lies a potential doctrine of pneumatology. A traditional understanding of the concept of God as Spirit is common to both Christianity and African traditional religion. Setiloane says: "It [God] manifests *Itself* in physical phenomena, such as lightning and thunder" (1976b, 80). This is why African theology believes both that God is spirit and that God's presence can be felt and experienced physically. African theology needs to explicate the doctrine of the Holy Spirit in such a way that believers may feel the tangibleness of the benefits of knowing Christ.

The commonest African concept of God is that God is regarded as the Creator. As Mbiti points out

> Practically all African people consider God as Creator, making this the commonest attribute of the works or activities of God. The concept is expressed through saying directly that God created all things, through giving him the name of Creator (or its equivalent), and through addressing him in prayer as the Creator or Maker [1970b, 45].

On this concept, every African theologian has something positive to say. Sawyerr's *God: Ancestor or Creator?* deals directly with this particular belief. The creation myths in the traditional worldview illustrate God as the Creator or Maker. With this concept African theologians must begin and end their task of theologizing.

Although there are numerous other African concepts of God, it is not necessary to discuss each one because our purpose is not to catalogue the many African ideas of God. Our concern is to show the importance of African traditional religion for those scholars who are seeking to develop an African theology. There can be no adequate discussion of the origin and development of African theology apart from a consideration, not only of the concept of God, but also of ancestral spirits in African religion.

THE CONCEPT OF ANCESTRY

African theologians are keenly interested in the concept of ancestral spirits, a major ingredient in African traditional religion and hence in African theology.

Harry Sawyerr describes the traditional African sense of the presence of the dead: "It is this fact of presence that has led to the belief in the continued existence of the ancestral spirits and in their influence on their descendants" (1968, 26). C. G. Baeta makes a similar observation (1968, 60). This presence of the ancestral spirits or their equivalent in any given community augments the African spiritual understanding of the community.

Ancestors occupy a significant place in traditional religion because they are believed to possess supernatural powers. Sawyerr observes that "the presence of the dead is assumed and invoked when the life of the tribe is threatened with disaster" (1968, 26). Many theologians support the view that: "Ancestors remain . . . spiritual superintendents of family affairs and continue to bear their titles of relationship like 'father' or 'mother' " (Idowu 1975, 184). African theologians can draw significant insights from the belief in ancestral spirits. The importance of this belief for both traditional religion and a developing theology lies in the fact that ancestrology properly places emphasis on the reality of the spirit world. For the African, Christian worship makes sense when it emphasizes a spiritual dimension. Moreover, Africans believe that the ancestors provide a link with the life-giving spirit world. According to Fashole-Luke:

> African theologians must therefore recover the practice of the ancient North African Church and pray in faith for the departed, both Christian and non-Christian. This will provide the Africans with that link with their dead which they so much desire [1974, 219].

It is almost universally held by African theologians that their people believe that the spiritual is just as important and consequential as the physical. Hence, a living human being can carry on a conversation with the spiritual or invisible living-dead (Mbiti 1970a, 11). That African traditional religion does not simply consist in the everyday physical realities but also involves spiritual realities is best dramatized in the prominent place given to the ancestors in worship and thought.[6] This fact makes African traditional religion a live background for a relevant theology.

Geoffrey Parrinder refers to this influence when he says that "all Ibo believe that their lives are profoundly influenced by their ancestors, and this belief has far-reaching sociological consequences" (1974, 57). A vital role of ancestors in African traditional religion is to hold the community together. Where ancestors are venerated, they are "factors of cohesion in African society" (Idowu 1975, 185). Some African theologians also contend that "the ancestors are the custodians of the morality of the tribe or community: hence ethical conduct is determined by reference to the ancestors" (Fashole-Luke 1974, 213). M. J. McVeigh writes:

> African attention is centered on the ancestors who are looked up to as the guardians of individuals, families, and the community as a whole. Those in flesh constantly seek communion with the departed [1974a, 103].

In the same vein, Pobee discusses the role of the ancestors as godly: "God the Supreme Being has delegated authority to the *abosom* (gods) and to the *mpanyinto* (the ancestors), who, therefore, act *in loco Dei* and *pro Dei* " (1979, 46). African theology can develop the doctrine of pneumatology within the framework of ancestrology, since the latter is understood to mediate between the biologically living and the spiritual realities, including God.

A significant point that needs to be highlighted is the cleansing process which the would-be ancestor goes through prior to installation. The Shona call this process *Chenura*. The community forgives the would-be ancestor of all sin committed even inadvertently. That ritual entitles the now "ancestor" to commune with the saints gone on before as well as to communicate with God at a spiritual level. Thus, when Africans talk of the ancestors as righteous and just, they also imply that ancestors are creatures that do not do any wrong and consequently are able to regulate morality in the community.

The importance of this for African theology lies in the light it sheds on the doctrine of sin. The people and God can work together in their respective capacities to cleanse, forgive, and therefore save the fallible human being. The ancestor then becomes a saint, charged by God with the responsibility of ensuring the welfare of the people of his or her own tribe.

The ancestors are believed to watch over their own folk. They seek to please and preserve their living relatives, provided that the latter pledge to appease their ancestors. The relationship is mutual and limited to the clan in question. This exclusive tendency of Africans is not necessarily a condemnation of other races. It is merely an attempt to affirm the culture of their own people. I believe that God chooses the agents, in this case the ancestors, who relate to a particular people and God works through those agents to save the people. It is in this sense that Pobee says: "There is a dependence of the living on the ancestors whose authority is nevertheless derived from God." Since the ancestors have been endowed with the power to enable African survival, Pobee concludes that "the attitude of the living toward the ancestors is something more than veneration" (1979, 47).

African theological concepts that are developed along the lines of ancestrology must necessarily address the question of survival which is wrought by God through the ancestors. The ancestral concepts establish a connection among the individual, the community, and God. In the other direction, too, God channels forgiveness through the community to the individual. Setiloane correctly explains how this phenomenon actually unfolds:

> A young man, wishing to make an approach to *MODIMO* [God], approaches his elder brother, who approaches his father, who approaches his grandfather . . . and the request is passed up the hierarchy of *badimo* until it reaches one sufficiently senior to address *MODIMO* directly [1976b, 65].

We can infer that ancestors should play a vital role in African theology because they are the way to God. African theology must reconcile this idea with the gospel's claim that Jesus is the Way. This presents a serious question. Is there any continuity between the two faiths? Is there more than one way to God?

For the African, these questions are significant because the two faiths need to be synchronized in a way that does not in any way jeopardize African existence. If anything, such plurality should enhance it. This integration is important for African theology because it leaves no possibility of a negative syncretism.[7]

African theology and ancestrology try to interpret historical events, such as a series of deaths in one family. However it is believed that the power to understand such events emanates from God. The ancestors are merely God's agents and creations. Also, Africans believe that their ancestors have the power to control and regulate cosmological cause and effect. Consequently African traditional religion upholds the belief that ancestors, if well-pleased, can make things go well for their living families. By the same token, if they are displeased, the ancestors may invoke evil on their families. Good and evil have profound ramifications among the Africans and are taken very seriously by traditional religion. In turn, theology must formulate its tenets according to these concepts.

THE CONCEPTS OF GOOD AND EVIL

Concepts of good and evil constitute a major part of traditional religion. Modern theologians may wish to develop an African decalogue that will regulate their people; they may develop ethics separate from theology. In either case, the importance of good and evil in traditional religion makes it a vital source for an African theology.

There are African creation myths like the biblical story of Eden that say that God created humanity and put the first group of people in paradise (Mbiti 1970b, 166). Everything was good in the beginning. In fact, some African tribes believe that "the first people lived happily, lacking nothing, as God provided them with food, shelter, and immortality" (Mbiti 1970b, 167). So when Africans do everything possible to avoid evil, or when they deal with it, they are seeking to capture that original ideal state. Unlike western theology and philosophy, which spend much time trying to establish the origin of evil, African traditional religion spends much time dealing with the causes and effects of evil (Pobee 1979, 99). An African theology that develops with this background may take the form of a problem-solving theology, rather than a problem-oriented theology.

Most African theologians who treat the subject of evil and good in an African cosmology agree that there is evil in this world. Evil is a reality, though it is not clear where it originates. Parrinder argues that some scholars believe that evil may be attributed to the ancestors (1974, 60). There are some African theologians, however, who differ with Parrinder, believing that evil has other human, spiritual, or natural forces as its agents. They make the point clear that the agent itself is basically not evil; it becomes evil insofar as it causes evil to happen. This view is consistent with the Bible, which teaches that everything that is was created by God and is therefore good.[8] African theology can evolve a doctrine of humanity that affirms the goodness of human nature, and may contribute vital insights to the doctrine of original sin.

That traditional religion has rituals that can control or cope effectively with evil when it occurs makes ritual very important for African theology. Sacrifice is one example, treated thoroughly by Harry Sawyerr (Dickson and Ellingworth 1971, 57). Traditional rituals can bring useful theological insights to the church today.

Pobee classifies evil according to its causes: the primary cause and the secondary cause (1979, 100). Witches are in the first category, while any other human being who does wrong belongs to the second category. The difference is that witches are possessed with evil involuntarily, while others decide to indulge in an evil act. African theologians agree with Pobee's view that "there is at one point or other, human responsibility or input into the occurrence of evil" (Pobee 1979, 100). This does not, however, make African humanity inherently evil. Even a witch is not evil by nature since, as a human being, she is good; she is evil insofar as the spirit of evil possesses her (Pobee 1979, 100). Thus in the African context, witchcraft is a practical, tangible example of evil that possesses a human being who is otherwise good. An African doctrine of humanity that is formulated in the light of this distinction between evil by nature and evil by possession can address the question of the problem of evil in a fresh manner.

Since the basic agents of evil are human persons, what, then, is the African concept of humanity? This classical question has occupied most African theologians.

THE CONCEPT OF HUMANITY

The concept of humanity, which has largely determined all other African cosmological concepts, is central in traditional religion. How African humanity has traditionally perceived itself is of primary importance to a developing African theology.

Mbiti summarizes the perspective of most African theologians:

Since African peoples consider the universe to be centered on man, it is to be expected that there would be more myths about man's own origin and early state than about anything else [1975a, 77].

It is therefore necessary to highlight the importance of humanity in both African traditional religion and African theology, the latter being a theological reflection upon the former. Elsewhere Mbiti informs us that "it is generally acknowledged that God is the originator of man, even if the exact methods of creating man may differ according to the myths of different peoples" (1970a, 120). Pobee finds it difficult to define African humanity because *"Homo Africanus* is a multiheaded hydra" (1979, 18). Yet, difficult though it may be to describe, Africans have a certain image of humanity that can be articulated.

In his article "The Theological Estimate of Man" (1969) Swailem Sidhom discusses the African view of humanity. Most theologians would agree with him that African humanity is defined in the context of the community. "All that goes into the making of man is incorporated in the complex unity of the tribe, outside of which all others are strangers and inferiors, if not enemies" (Sidhom 1969, 99). This means that any outsider is likely to violate tribal folkways and mores, causing chaos and catastrophies in the community. Foreigners are considered enemies because their motives are likely to be alien to the local tribal interest. Moreover, their loyalties are bound to be elsewhere. All these unknowns threaten peace in the community. So we find that African humanity is primarily defined by a sense of belonging, serving one's own folk, and kinship. For the African, it is not enough to be a human being; unless one shares a sense of community, one can easily turn out to be an enemy.

African theology may derive the criteria for belonging to a community of believers from this traditional concept of humanity in community. Such a definition of the community of believers takes collective survival very seriously. Thus two major concerns of African theology, solidarity and humanization, find clear expression in the context of the community.

Most African scholars agree that in traditional religion humanity is to be conceived as "being in relation." In the words of Mercy Oduyoye:

Africans recognize life as life-in-community. We can truly know ourselves if we remain true to our community, past and present. The concept of individual success or failure is secondary. The ethnic group, the village, the locality, are crucial in one's estimation of oneself. Our nature as beings-in-relation is a two-way relation: with God and with our fellow human beings [1979, 110–111].

One is defined in one's own social context, namely one's community.

Among my people, the Shona, every piece of property in the community is referred to as *vedu* or *chedu*, a possessive pronoun that means "ours" as opposed to "mine." This applies even to parents. Under normal circumstances, one would never say *Baba wangu* (my father). One is more apt to say *Baba vedu* (our father).[9] Thus, the individual understands himself or herself in the context of the community, or at least the family.

Strains of Western thought which have been influenced by Descartes's "I think, therefore I am" (*cogito ergo sum*) and Albert Camus's "I rebel—therefore we exist" (Camus 1956, 22) contrast with African concepts of humanity. The concept of humanity in the African context as described by Mbiti places the emphasis elsewhere.

> Whatever happens to the individual happens to the whole group, and whatever happens to the whole group happens to the individual. The individual can only say: "I am, because we are and since we are, therefore I am" [1970a, 141].

This is the key to the understanding of the African view of humanity, and, in Mbiti's words, "a cardinal point in the understanding of the African view of man" (1970a, 141). "Nature brings the child into the world, but society creates the child into a social being, a corporate person" (1970a, 143). Thus African culture is the proper context in which African humanity can be fully comprehended. This is why most African theologians contend that doing African theology should be a process of Africanization. This is possible only if the theology is developed in the context of African traditional religion, which is itself an integral part of the culture.

Since African views of humanity are expressed in religious concepts via traditional religion, African theologians have treasured their religious heritage.

SUMMARY

The effectiveness of African theology depends on how indigenous it is. African traditional religion provides African theology with a theological framework within which the latter can develop. A theology that incorporates basic concepts of the tradition and is congenial to African beliefs will be more relevant to the needs of Africans than a theology expressed in borrowed concepts.

We have discussed the concept of God in traditional life and have seen how African theological concepts of God are being formulated within the traditional theological frame. One of the very important features to bear in mind is that most African theologians agree that numerous Africans acknowledge the one God whose self-manifestation occurs in different ways to different individuals and communities. General revelation that may include special revelation provides African theology with a firm, indigenous doctrine of God that is consistent with African beliefs and with the essence of the gospel.

We have ascertained also how belief in the ancestral spirits sheds light on the doctrine of forgiveness as well as on the idea of life-after-death and the communion of saints. Ancestrology provides a useful framework for the construction of an African Christology because it deals with life beyond mere physical existence. We have also seen that ancestrology adds a spiritual dimension to our understanding of humanity and is a factor in making a community cohere. Therefore, an African doctrine of humanity draws heavily on the traditional doctrine of ancestrology.

We have tried to locate the source of evil as the Africans understand it. African theology can formulate theological concepts that relate to the problem of theodicy, a problem that has been of great concern in Christendom. African traditional religion holds that all good comes from God and that evil was not created by God. Without an agent, evil has no effect. We have also discussed the importance of the concept of goodness among the Africans. We have seen that evil and good among the Africans are not abstractions but concrete realities. An African theology that is constructed with this background makes tangible rather than abstract statements about truth, love, God, and similar concepts.

To summarize, African traditional religion is important for the development of African theology in these four ways:

1. In reconciling general and special revelation, African theology can develop concepts that combine the particularity and the generality of the presence of God.

2. It gives the believer some light beyond physical existence. Ancestrology illuminates the mystery of life-after-death. In redefining eschatology to mean a spiritual reality in the here-and-now, traditional religion enables African theology to affirm spiritual beings in the present life, and not just in the afterlife.

3. It has a relatively healthy approach to, and understanding of, theodicy.

4. It defines humanity in such a way that only humanizing principles must be adopted in African life.

Finally, although African traditional religion and Christianity are not the same, and need not be, they do share major religious concerns such as the knowledge of God, spiritual existence, good-and-evil, and humanity.

Based on the preceding discussion, my belief is that African theology will be capable of dealing with present African realities. It will express the presence of God as well as absolute human dependence on God, and will acknowledge the susceptibility of humanity to both good and evil.

However, when the missionaries brought Christianity to the Africans, somehow African traditional religion was almost completely submerged, and even condemned, because it did not teach about Jesus Christ, the Son of God. In the next chapter, we discuss the coming of Christianity to Africa and the impact of the new faith on the African people.

Chapter 2

The Coming of Christianity to Africa: The Nineteenth and Twentieth Centuries

Most African theologians agree that there would have been no written African theology if the white missionaries had not brought the Bible. Consequently, interest in the origin and development of African theology necessitates a thorough understanding of the planting of Christianity in Africa.

Our discussion in this chapter will focus on the coming of Christianity to Africa and its impact on that continent during the nineteenth and twentieth centuries. Theologians believe that the impact of Christianity on the African people was so phenomenal that it is largely responsible for the present quest for an African theology (Fashole-Luke 1975, 259).

Both present-day missionaries and native Christians have shown interest in the impact of Christianity in Africa and much has been written recently on Christianity and African culture and religions. T. A. Beetham's *Christianity and the New Africa* discusses the coming of Christianity to Africa. *A New Look at Christianity in Africa* juxtaposes Christianity and African culture. The two volumes entitled *Christianity South of the Zambezi*, edited by A. J. Dachs and M. F. C. Bourdillon, discuss the coming of Christianity into southern Africa and the Africans' response to Christianity.

The collection of essays *Christianity in Tropical Africa*, edited by C. G. Baeta, also treats the planting of Christianity and how the Africans received it. It covers various aspects of Anglophone and Francophone Africa. Adrian Hastings has written two books on Christianity in Africa: *African Christianity* and *A History of African Christianity 1950–1975*. Bishop B. G. M. Sundkler's *The Christian Ministry in Africa* has been selected as a textbook by some African theological colleges. This book is a pioneer attempt at Africanizing Christianity. Mbiti has written articles along the same line, notably "The Encounter of Christian Faith and African Religion." Most African theologians acknowledge that the coming of Christianity to Africa is as important for the discussion of the origin and development of African theology as is African traditional religion.

The majority of African theological scholars are Christian believers interested in indigenizing the faith. In most cases they are themselves first or second generation Christians, and they stand so close to the coming of Christianity that they can testify personally to its impact in Africa today.[1] For instance, all these theologians agree that the Scriptures (which are the basis of Christianity) are fundamental to any theology that would be Christian.[2]

If, then, the Bible is indispensable for African theology, several questions arise: How did it come to the continent of Africa? What impact did Christianity have on the African people? To answer these questions, I shall discuss the activities of some missionary societies, how they "planted" Christianity in Africa, and its impact on the African peoples.

Most African theologians see the presence of Christianity in Africa in three stages: the infant Jesus as a refugee in Egypt; Christianity in Africa "under the Portuguese prowess of the fifteenth to the seventeenth century";[3] and, finally, the dramatic nineteenth-century awakening (Lugira n.d., 53). We are interested in the third stage because it has made an indelible impression on the African people to date.

I shall describe the planting of Christianity in Africa in two phases: first, the background and the launching of Christianity by various missionary societies and, second, the impact of Christianity on the African people. Throughout, I hope to bring to the surface the importance of the planting of Christianity for an African theology as well as to describe the impact of the new faith.

THE HISTORICAL BACKGROUND
OF THE MISSIONARY SOCIETIES

The factors that are largely responsible for the spread of Christianity in modern Africa are the great eighteenth-century religious revivals, the wake of the colonial era, and obedience to the gospel.

According to John Dillenberger and Claude Welch, Christianity came to Africa south of the Sahara as a large-scale Protestant missionary activity. This movement was aroused by William Carey's book *An Enquiry into the Obligations of Christians to Use Means for the Conversion of the Heathens*, which was published in 1872. In fact, there is general agreement in Protestant circles that "the nineteenth century was the period of the greatest geographic spread of Christianity" (Dillenberger and Welch 1954, 166). It was then that Christianity was planted permanently in sub-Saharan Africa. And it is there that African theology has been undertaken since the mid-twentieth century.

Hastings gives partial credit for the spread of Christianity to the freed African slaves.

The men who really carried the Christian faith along the West Coast in the mid-nineteenth century were nearly all Africans, many of them men and women rescued from the slave ships on the Atlantic and landed by the British navy at Freetown, in Sierra Leone [1977, 2].

This combination of Christian endeavors and commerce was characteristic of most of the missionary era. I will elucidate this point when discussing the missionary style of planting Christianity.

Many missionary activities were undertaken by Europeans and Americans. According to Dillenberger and Welch, "The appearance in Protestantism of a new and pervasive impulse to carry the gospel to all men began to take serious hold early in the nineteenth century" (1954, 169). These authors agree that a "religious understanding which lay behind the missionary impulse had its roots in the revivals of the eighteenth and early nineteenth centuries" (171).

From these revivals, many felt the need to respond to the "authority of the Scriptures." Some were inspired by the gospel to follow the example of the earliest Christians. Some felt a "heightened sense of the nearness of God's Kingdom." Others were motivated to "make actual the universality of the church" (172). In short, "the concern for missionary work came increasingly to be seen as the natural and inevitable response of faith to the revelation of God in Christ" (172). As a consequence, various missionary societies were formed or revived (if they had already existed) to serve in the mission field.

THE MISSIONARY STYLE OF PLANTING CHRISTIANITY

Scholars agree that "the first European missionaries were the Portuguese," who brought the gospel to Africa under the auspices of the See of Rome. "Priests generally accompanied the expeditions. They served as chaplains to the new trading settlements and as missionaries to neighboring African peoples" (Beetham 1967, 7–8). This was a cheaper method for the not-so-rich missionary societies to penetrate the interior of Africa. However, in the long run, this style created a rather unfortunate confusion.

John Mbiti agrees with Beetham that the white European missionaries worked together with the colonial groups. "We must note that Christian missionaries from Europe and America penetrated into the interior of Africa either shortly before or simultaneously with colonial occupation" (1970a, 302). Beetham says that most local Christian outreach often started from "these trading posts." He also notes that "missionaries were often led to make one town rather than another their center through the urging of some ship's captain, himself a member of their church back home" (1967, 11). The important point to bear in mind here is that the planting of Christianity occurred simultaneously with colonization. Consequently, there is a thin line between the missionary intention and the intent of the colonizers. I presume that missionaries only meant to take advantage of the health and transportation facilities made available by the colonizers, but not to facilitate colonization as such. What is indisputable is the fact that the colonists tended to use the missionaries to make their task easier.

In Zvobgo's article on Methodist missions in Rhodesia (now Zimbabwe), he states:

The representative of the society [The Wesleyan Methodist Missionary Society] came to the newly occupied country with Rhodes' encouragement, when he offered on behalf of the British South Africa company £ 100 per annum towards the expenses of a missionary who would serve in a new country [1973, 174].

This clearly implies that, in some instances, Christianity came to Africa with the active assistance of the settlers and traders. Hence confusion resulted as to the intentions of the missionaries and those of the colonizers.

Dillenberger and Welch remind us that this type of collaboration between church and state can be traced back to the Roman Empire during Constantine's rule.

When Christianity had become the established religion of the empire, the propagation of the faith had been actively sponsored by the rulers of Christian countries. This had continued to be true of the expansion in the sixteenth to eighteenth centuries, when the work of the Roman Catholic missionaries was strongly supported by governments of Spain and Portugal, and Orthodox missionaries by the Russian Government [1954, 174].

Although in the wake of the separation of church and state in countries like the United States of America such help was no longer forthcoming (Dillenberger and Welch 1954, 174), this lack of financial support did not mean that there was a lack of other kinds of support among the Euro-American churches and governments. In his article entitled "The Predicament of the Church in Africa" (Baeta 1968), E. B. Idowu documents the fact that respective governments supported the missionary societies originating from their nations. If they did not give financial aid, at least they gave moral support. For instance, Idowu tells us that "When the C.M.S. missionary arrived at the court of Mutesa I of Buganda, he presented two letters of commendation, one from the Church Missionary Society, and another from the Foreign Office." He adds that "The C.M.S. in Sierra Leone actually received an annual subsidy of £ 500 from the government for over a period and this is a common feature of missionary work all over Africa" (Baeta 1968, 423).

I, myself, know of a missionary who served as a police reservist during the white minority rule in Rhodesia.[4] Thus I can confirm Idowu's report that some missionaries served as "liaison officers between the Colonial Government and the people. Some of them became part-time civil servants. And some even fought in a war of supremacy between tribes" (Baeta 1968, 424).

Such facts as these are often cited in support of allegations made by Africans that some missionaries were being paid by their governments to assist in colonization. While Africans responded to the material aspects of the missionaries' message, they did not make a deep commitment to the religion practiced by white people who colonized and oppressed them.

Today many African theologians are concerned to formulate a genuine African theology because Christianity has remained foreign to African believers. Perhaps African Christians received the new faith with a grain of salt. As long as Africans remain split between two faiths, we cannot expect either religion to take hold seriously, nor should we blame either one for not being efficacious.

The planting of Christianity in Africa in its various forms was often strongly culturally oriented. Accordingly, the mark of a "saved" African was whether he or she had assimilated certain elements of Western culture (Price 1968, 108). Clearly the essence of the gospel became synonymous with Western culture in the thinking of the new convert. The danger in this apparent historical coincidence and confusion is that "the image that Africans received, and to a great extent still hold, of Christianity is very much colored by colonial rule and all that was involved in it" (Mbiti 1970a, 302). It is within the context of the negative impact of colonialism that African scholars rightly contend that what Africa needs is the essence of Christianity without the Western cultural garb in which the new faith was wrapped when it was first preached in Africa (Appiah-Kubi 1974, 5).

Some scholars claim that any African theology that develops from a colonial background must be colored by colonialism and its ramifications. The style of the planting of Christianity does in fact affect the character of African theology. But the point I wish to make is this: these shortcomings can never minimize the significance of the contribution of missionaries who introduced Africans to the Bible and its message.

THE MISSIONARY GROUPS
AND THEIR MOTIVATION

The most important document that missionaries brought to Africa was the Bible. No other document has done more to influence the character of African Christianity and its theology. Most African Christians regard the Bible as God's written word, and African theologians who are concerned about African theology accept the claim of the Pan-African Conference of Third World Theologians that

> the Bible is the basic source of African theology, because it is the primary witness of God's revelation in Jesus Christ. No theology can retain its Christian identity apart from Scripture [Appiah-Kubi and Torres 1979, 81].

It seems clear that the primary motive of the missionaries who brought the Christian faith to Africa was to bring the good news, the message of salvation. First, we must acknowledge the contribution made by the African ex-slaves who settled in Freetown, Sierra Leone. These African Christians spread the message of salvation in many countries of West Africa. As a result of this spontaneous missionary movement, "Christian congregations were to be found in many coastal towns in the Gambia, the Gold Coast, Dahomey and Nigeria" (Beetham 1967, 10). Out of this context emerged people like Samuel Ajayi Crowther (Sundkler 1960, 46), an African convert who was later consecrated and became the first African Anglican bishop in the Church of Western Africa (*Journal* 1855). Once African leadership was trained and equipped with the gospel, the seed of the church was sown in African soil. The origin of African theology can be traced back to those early days when the Christian message was first received by the first-generation Christians.

The rest of the missionary movements in Africa were initiated and conducted by both European and American white missionaries, assisted, as we have noted, by traders and colonists. For our purposes, I will discuss the activities of only the major missionary societies, for my emphasis is rather on the general message that the missionaries brought to Africa.

In southern Africa one of the leading societies was the London Missionary Society (L.M.S.), which was established in 1795. It arose "from the English evangelical revival of the late eighteenth century." The motivation of the L.M.S. was "promoting 'the great work of introducing the Gospel and its ordinances to heathen and other unenlightened countries.' " The members of the Society "avowed as their 'sole object' . . . to spread the knowledge of Christ among the heathen" and to propagate " 'the glorious Gospel of the blessed God' " (Dachs 1973, 53).

The Wesleyan Methodist Missionary Society (W.M.M.S.) from Britain established churches in West and Southern Africa. Its motive was similar to that of the London Missionary Society, namely, to convert the sinner and bring the message of salvation to the African peoples (Dachs 1973, 54). John de Gruchy notes that Protestant missionaries "arrived by the score from Europe and America 'to Christianize the heathen' " (de Gruchy 1979, 21). African theologians who acknowledge the importance of Christianity for African theology take this "salvation theme" as the basic message, thus making Christ central in their work.

The Roman Catholic Society of African Missions began its work in 1859 (Beetham 1967, 11). It started its missionary activities at Freetown, as did several other European and American societies. The R.C.S.A.M. was founded by Bishop de Bresillac but its work was done mainly by Africans. Beetham notes that, due to the white people's weak resistance to disease, the Society was forced to indigenize its missions. Consequently, African preachers and evangelists were trained to serve parts of the continent which the Euro-Americans could not reach. This health problem turned out to be a blessing in disguise, since the new strategy produced influential African Christians like Crowther of Nigeria, Charles Knight of Sierra Leone, J. P. Brown and F. C. Grant of Ghana, who were exceptionally good preachers (Beetham 1967, 12).

The Liberian city of Monrovia was another point of entry. However, the city was not as suitable a "trading post" as Freetown, where Christian communities of ex-slaves were liberally planted by the Americans. Most churches were established there under American initiative, both Protestant and Roman Catholic. Even though Monrovia was not a very suitable "trading post," years later (1914) from there emerged one of Africa's greatest traveling evangelists, William Wadé Harris.[5]

In East Africa the major European missionary group was the Church Missionary Society. This party of German missionaries "reached Zanzibar in 1844" (Beetham 1967, 14) and proceeded to Uganda in 1877. Another group of Catholic missionaries, coming from North Africa, arrived in Uganda about 1879. Although these pioneer missionaries were subjected to heavy persecution and even death,[6] Beetham tells us that in no time "Christians had become the major political force in the country by the time colonial rule began in 1894" (1967, 14).

Like other missionary societies, they preached the good news that Christ died so that they might have eternal life. On the west coast of Africa, the Baptist Missionary Society (B.M.S.) "entered the Congo in 1870, to be followed by the first significant group of independent missionaries" (Beetham 1967, 14). The French Holy Ghost Fathers began to serve in Senegal in 1843, and by 1866, they had penetrated the mainland of Angola and part of the Congo (Beetham 1967, 15).

All these groups had a common goal, namely, to evangelize the heathen. Furthermore, each group expected to convert the natives not only spiritually, but culturally as well. Unless the African pagans adopted much of Western culture and civilization, it was difficult to measure the success of the missionary task. David Livingstone summed up this missionary expectation when he remarked on indirect results in the southern African context:

> If we call the actual amount of conversions the direct result of missions, and wide diffusion of better principles the indirect, the latter are of infinitely more importance than the former [Dachs 1973, 54].

Along the same line of thought, Anthony Chennells notes that: "To the early missionaries in the century, the adoption of European life styles by the heathen was regarded as one of the fruits of conversion to Christianity" (Chennells 1973, 43).

In a lecture delivered at the University of Cambridge in 1857, David Livingstone said: "I went into that country for the purpose of teaching the doctrines of our holy religion" (Monk 1818, 145). But the same Livingstone also bluntly declared that he would be going to Africa to open the continent for both commerce and Christianity. T. Price interprets this to mean that Livingstone

> was outlining his strategy first for strangling the slave trade, in the interest of the bodily survival of the Africans; and then for making the life thus obtained for them worth living [Price 1968, 101].

My personal inference is that David Livingstone believed in both spiritual and physical freedom. It appears that Livingstone held the view that unless the African heathens were physically free from slavery, spiritual salvation would not mean much to them. This concept of holistic freedom is an important ingredient in the origin and development of African theology.

The principal target of the missionary in Africa was the devil. According to Aylward Shorter, "early missionaries saw the devil everywhere" in Africa. "In missionary eyes mission lands were the 'Empire of Satan' " (1974, 21). Thus the central message brought by the missionaries to Africa was salvation from, first, an unchristian cultural life style, second, bondage by the devil, and, third, the darkness of not knowing God and Jesus Christ. In short, Africa needed to be redeemed from being the "Empire of Satan."

All over the continent, mission stations were set up like little colonies. Most African scholars agree with Shorter's analysis that a mission settlement was "a world apart from the village-world of the people. People came to the mission, not the mission to the people" (Shorter 1974, 22). How could Christians mix with the people of the mission lands who, as Shorter puts it, "in practice . . . were damned— in the grip of Satan himself" (1974, 21)?

In spite of inconsistencies and paradoxes, the white missionaries showed great dedication to the African heathens. The Christian love of the missionaries for the Africans made up for the former's undesirable association and collaboration with the colonialists. Aylward Shorter writes:

> If the early missionaries had not been spiritual giants they would not have got away with what they did, but they were holy men, of immense courage and personality. . . . People speak of them today with love and admiration, and are proud of them though they disagree with some of the things they did [1974, 24].

We may conclude that the Christian message was received by the Africans in spite of the shortcomings of the missionaries who proclaimed it. Apparently, the denominational differences did not bother the African people.

Protestants and Roman Catholics participated in the planting of Christianity in their respective regions. On the Protestant side, there were the well-established denominations, such as the Lutheran, the Dutch Reformed Church, the Presbyterians, the Anglicans, the Baptists, the Methodists, and the Congregationalists. On the Roman Catholic side, several missionary orders participated. However, as time went on, these two strands subdivided into numerous subsections. We will not discuss these divisions because that is not our primary task. Suffice it to note that the faith had been planted.

THE IMPACT OF CHRISTIANITY ON THE AFRICAN PEOPLE

Christianity has been a tremendous socioreligious influence on the African people. In fact, most African theologians would agree with Peter Sarpong's statement that "when cultures encounter each other, there is bound to be impact of one upon another" (n.d., 25). In discussing the origin of African theology, it is important that I describe the impression Christianity made upon the African. The impact of the white presence was especially felt and is evident in the social, economic, and religious aspects of African life.

In this regard Professor Baeta is correct to state that "missionaries were by no means merely evangelists and prophets. They were also leaders to whom the African communities looked for introduction to the highly complex new ways of life bursting in upon them, as well through the missionary's own coming as through the other channels of government and trade." In fact, he goes on, "the mission station was not merely a base for teaching the Christian discipline and manner of living and for propagating the Faith: it was also a pocket of this new invading civilization, displaying and mediating a wide range of its techniques" (Baeta 1968, 15).

The African converts had to adjust to the new way of life. The missionary-trained Africans, who had become literate, changed their means of earning a living when the colonial administrators hired them as civil servants. Over a few decades, the African breadwinner began to feel that a large family was not an asset but a financial burden in a cash economy. This new attitude was a clear departure from the traditional view that cherished a large family. Thus, the institution of the family was immediately affected by the presence of Christianity as it was presented in Western garb. Polygamy was despised by the missionaries so much that African converts began to condemn it too. In fact, present-day missionaries like Aylward Shorter still insist that monogamy, and not polygamy, is the Christian ideal (1974, 174), arguing this position from the Book of Genesis (2:24).[7] Those in favor of polygamy, on the other hand, cite the story of Jacob and his two wives, Leah and Rachel, and contend that polygamy is biblical too. But such a claim is classified as backward; worse still, it is labeled unchristian.

Christianity also made a direct impact on the African lifestyle by the introduction of formal education. As N .M. B. Bhebe has put it, "Civilization in its simplest and most practical form meant the adoption, by Africans, of European behavior, food, clothing, and other Western customs" (1973, 45). In the process of its development, African theology takes such issues as the family in general and polygamy in particular for theological explication. With the help of African theology, believers must articulate what makes a cultural practice "Christian" or "non-Christian."

Christianity was presented in such a way that the African was made to believe that he or she had to go through social metamorphosis before becoming acceptable in God's sight. The early missionaries were inclined to think that most African practices and customs were unchristian and consequently wrong. A case in point is the African marriage system.

Fr. Prestage, S.J., a British missionary, denounced the African marriage system because it was

> the purchase of a wife by a man for the purpose of begetting children, among whom the girls, when marriageable, are disposed of to obtain *lobola,* which is used again to purchase other wives, the final object being to acquire position and substance through possession of women and children [Bhebe 1973, 45].

Fr. Prestage was convinced that there was no love in an African marriage. I would submit that there is need for an African theology that will critically reflect upon the African concepts of love, procreation, and community in the light of the gospel.

The material abundance of the early missionaries made a great economic impact on the African people. Africans were impressed by the quality and quantity of Western materialism. It is reported that

> in commercial wares brought by Europeans, in their bearing and comportment, there was every sign of wealth, and of this wealth Africans were already having a taste in the gifts brought to them by explorers. The general impression was great and arresting [Baeta, 1968, 423].

Consequently, Christianity appeared for most Africans to be a religion of material abundance. Material wealth was one sign of spiritual blessedness for most African converts. Because of this interpretation, many Africans converted to Christianity in order to be prosperous. Anthony J. Dachs says of a British missionary in Southern Africa that: "U. Read simply settled with Mothibi in December 1816 and won the chief's support and that of his immediate family by providing them with favors and gifts, including a gun" (Dachs 1973, 55). Along this vein, allow me to draw on an illustration from my own family. My mother, who is a first-generation Christian, told me that in her teens, she and her peers were enticed by the American missionaries to go to school by being given sugar to lick every day if they attended lessons. The point is that Western materialism was often used to effectively induce a positive attitude toward Western culture and values.

Spiritual salvation was advertised through material possessions, especially imported Western goods. Idowu observes that Christianity was presented and understood as "a religion with a prestige value" (Baeta 1968, 424). The Africans who had received salvation had also been taught to read and write. Consequently, they got well-paying civil positions and became well-to-do, proving that those who were saved automatically became better off materially. Later on, when the Africans started to fight for their God-given land, the missionaries changed the criterion for salvation. This time, poverty was the sign of the true people of God. Idowu says that, surrounded by the Western cultural matrix, Christianity tended to become coterminous with Western civilization. "Westernism and Christianity became mixed up" (Baeta 1968, 425).

The result of this economic impact was that "converts to Christianity despised their own cultures preferring European customs" (Baeta 1968, 425). A case in point is the impact of the Portuguese in the Congo. After missionaries had evangelized for some decades,

the King of Congo was asked to throw away all that might remind him of the old ways. Before long, a Portuguese veneer had spread over Congolese Society: Portuguese dress was adopted, Portuguese names were given at baptism, the King's capital city was renamed San Salvador, and the feudal system was introduced into the Court [Baeta 1968, 424].

The task of African theology is to deal with two elements simultaneously. It must reckon with African culture in its fractured state, and it must reckon with the distorted essence of Christianity. The two must be studied side by side in order to produce an African theology. This is why both the Bible and African traditional religion are sources for African theology.

Christianity's greatest effect was on African traditional religion. Most theologians would not dispute this obvious fact. Its effects in the areas discussed above might have been incidental, but the intent of the missionary movement was to make a religious impact. The mission was to convert the Africans from the darkness of not knowing God to Jesus Christ, the Light of the World (John 8:12).

Missionaries brought Christianity to Africa because they believed that Africans either had no religion or their religion was not true. We know today that both views are wrong.

I would agree with Idowu that "the European missionary came to Africa with the preconceived notion that there was either no religion at all in Africa or that it was entirely of the Devil" (Baeta 1968, 424). But, true or not, this notion is not the primary concern of this study. The important fact is that Africans knew God, but they did not know God's son, Jesus Christ. As my own father always told me, "The only new thing the missionaries brought to Africa is Jesus Christ, not God. We knew God."[8] Thus the impact of the missionary message of salvation was peculiarly *Christian,* not merely religious. This means that African theology has to reckon with the fact of Christ, formulating an African doctrine of the Trinity to clear this matter.

African theology can be Christian only if it is centered on Christ and his redemptive work. I have described the socioreligious background against which an African theology is being developed. The next two chapters on the independent church movement and African nationalism emanate from the encounter of Western civilization with African culture. Both movements are bound to retain an element of reaction and protest against the white presence in Africa until African theology sets the record straight. That is an enormous responsibility.

Chapter 3

The African Independent Church Movement

The African independent church movement[1] may be regarded by most African theologians as one of the few major sources of an African theology. What draws the attention and interest of the African theologians toward the African independent churches is the latter's tendency to indigenize the Christian faith. In two important respects the independent churches provide African scholars with material for an African theology: their emphasis on spirituality and faith-healing practices, and indigenization of the Christian doctrines and liturgies.

Before I discuss these two aspects I need to examine briefly the literary heritage of the independent church movement and make some general observations about the movement in Africa. One limitation here is that not much has been written by the participants of independency themselves. Most of the books on the movement have been written by authors other than African theologians. Nevertheless, these works give the necessary material and a framework for the formulation of an African theology. A good example is Bengt Sundkler's *Bantu Prophets in South Africa*, in which the author gives a comprehensive analysis of the sociological and religious problems of the South African separatist churches (1961, 13). Sundkler also wrote *The Christian Ministry in Africa*, a study which gives us invaluable information pertinent to the origins and development of an African theology. Chapter 5 in that book actually discusses what the author calls "Christian Theology in Africa." Most theologians agree with Sundkler's statement that

African theology "has to interpret . . . Christ in terms that are relevant and essential to African existence" (1960, 99). This is the basic concern of the African independent church movement and it is the reason some scholars believe that African theology originated in that movement. David Barrett's *Schism and Renewal in Africa* provides numerous examples demonstrating how the African independent churches became a major source. According to Mbiti:

> Barrett sees the movement of the Independent Churches as bringing into being an area of African theology. . . . According to him, these Independent Churches constitute an African Reformation and it is out of this that an African Theology emerges [1972b, 86].

Barrett himself sets as his goal to demonstrate "how creatively Africa can respond to the Christian faith when foreign assistance and (as some would add) foreign interference are withdrawn" (1968, xvii).

Hastings's work, *A History of African Christianity*, treats the African independent church movement as well as mission churches quite thoroughly. It, therefore, deserves a special place in the development of African theology. Geoffrey Parrinder has also written a book, *Religion in Africa*, in which he has devoted a whole chapter to independency as a historical phenomenon with theological ramifications. Several other non-African authors have written case studies of the African independent churches. M. L. Daneel's *Old and New in Southern Shona Independent Churches* focuses on a particular region in Zimbabwe. He discusses the recruitment techniques among the Vapostori and other Zionist-oriented movements in the Fort Victoria area. He has also written *Zionism and Faith-Healing in Rhodesia*. Because Daneel's work is primarily descriptive, African theologians can readily engage in theological reflection on the sermons that precede faith-healing sessions and other prophetic activities.

An emphasis on spirituality can be seen in C. G. Baeta's book, *Prophetism in Ghana*, G. M. Halliburton's *The Prophet Harris*, and M. L. Martin's *Kimbangu: An African Prophet and His Church*. All these works are case studies that emphasize spirituality in the indigenization of the faith, providing the African theologians with raw materials for African theology.

The independent church movement, though a relatively recent phenomenon, is rich in possibilities for the development of Christian doctrines that are relevant to the African church. For example, J.

Omoyajowo, in describing why indigenous churches came about and suggesting how African theologians can use this raw material in doing theology, writes: "The Holy Spirit descended and called out Africans to express Christianity in languages that would be understandable and meaningful to the people" (1972, 9). In *Post-Christianity in Africa*, G. C. Oosthuizen makes a systematic classification of the independent churches. Included in his treatment is not only a historical description of what they are, but also a theological interpretation of what they believe.

Edmund Ilogu discusses the emergence, challenge, and importance of the African independent churches (1970, 492–7), showing how they influence the origin and development of African theology. In discussing possible relationships that could emerge between the independent churches and the older churches, he points out that independency is concerned about African nationalism, interpretation of visions and dreams, orthodox faith, and the reinterpretation of Christ (1970, 497).

I do not intend to make an exposition of independency, but will discuss its emergence in order to establish its importance for African theology.

THE EMERGENCE OF INDEPENDENCE

Independent churches grew in the context either of mission churches or other indigenous churches. Thus it is not by accident that most of them were located in areas where the oldest mission churches had been established. Most scholars would agree with Hastings's observation that

it was some of the oldest areas of sustained Protestant missionary work which by 1950 had become the home of the most marked independency: South Africa, the West Africa coast, the Congo basin, Central Kenya [1979, 67].

A similar point is made by Geoffrey Parrinder.

The first independent movements began in West and South Africa in the nineteenth century, and they were followed by similar schisms in Central and East Africa before the end of the century [1969, 149].

We may note that it is also in these areas that African theology is being formulated. We need, however, to establish the reasons for the emergence of this phenomenon of independency and then see how it fosters the beginnings of African theology.

Parrinder argues that independent churches appeared in these particular regions first, not only because they wished to enjoy "freedom from foreign control," but also because they sought to carry on with "the evangelization of Africa by modern methods" (1969, 149). Two factors implicit here are indigenization and the spiritualization of Christianity. It is interesting that African theology is developing along the same lines.

Edmund Ilogu informs us that independent churches in West Africa "fall into two basic categories: Aladuraism and Ethiopianism" (1970, 492). Generally speaking, the former tends to be spiritually motivated,[2] while the latter is oriented politically.[3] Since both groups were founded by Africans who protested against the ecclesiastical status quo, they may be characterized also as independent churches. Furthermore, the leadership, as well as the membership, tends to be exclusively African. Although this pattern is more commonly found in West Africa, there is evidence of it throughout the continent.

In general "Ethiopianism" prevails where ethnic politics is a crucial issue. This explains why the first "Ethiopian" church[4] was "founded on the Witwaterstrand [South Africa] in 1892" (Sundkler 1961, 38). It was founded by Mangena M. Mokone, a malcontented African Wesleyan Methodist minister. He, together with others, seceded from the mission church structure because he "opposed what he regarded as racial segregation within the church, as seen by there being one conference for European leaders, and another for African leaders." Political consciousness is unmistakable here, as well as a genuine concern for unity under the same Lord. Mokone's views reflect those of other African independent church leaders. He withdrew from the mission church so that he might realize "self-government of the African Church under African leaders" (Sundkler 1961, 39). Shortly afterwards, he was succeeded by Dwane. Probably the main reason for the secession was not hostility; rather, Mokone and other African Christian leaders were seeking the best means to spread the good news. They were looking for a theology that was relevant to the needs of the African people.

Another example may help to illustrate this point. In Parrinder's words, "The first move was by a modest United Native African Church in Lagos, founded not as an alternative to the missions but as a more effective means of evangelism" (1969, 150). Omoyajowo's general impression is that "these movements 'sought to establish the

Christianity of the Bible as they saw it, devoid of its European accretions and in harmony with Africa's cultural heritage' " (1972, 9). It is a similar concern for an indigenized faith that draws African theologians to the independent churches in the quest for a relevant theology.

Besides the Witwaterstrand Church, there were other Ethiopian churches founded in South Africa during this period. In 1898, P. J. Mzimba founded the African Presbyterian Church, and Brander founded the Ethiopian Catholic Church in Zion in 1904, breaking away from another Ethiopian church, the African Methodist Episcopal Church (Sundkler 1961, 42). Numerous secessions occurred also within the Congregational churches. All these secessions in South Africa were politically motivated, hence the designation "Ethiopianism."

Hastings and Ilogu have characterized other independent churches as "the spirit churches." In South Africa, they are referred to as "Zionist."[5] Authorities designate the Zionist churches in West Africa, especially in Nigeria, as "Aladura" (Hastings 1979, 67–68; Peel 1968).

It is clear that whether in South Africa or in West Africa, the Zionist and the Aladura are basically "spirit-oriented." These spirit churches take on different names in other parts of Africa.[6] Their common characteristic is an emphasis on the spiritual life of their members and of the church as a whole. They stress pastoral ministry and the Holy Spirit is their norm. As I will demonstrate later, this high spirituality was lacking in the mission churches.

These "spirit churches" emphasized "satisfying Africa's spiritual thirst." The Liberian prophet Wadé Harris rose to prominence in 1913 and 1914 in the Ivory Coast and influenced the founding of "the Church of the Twelve Apostles in Western Ghana" (Parrinder 1969, 151) because he preached in such a way that the gospel quenched the congregation's spiritual thirst. Oosthuizen also has observed that that church "traces its origin to the Grebo (*kru*) prophet William Wadé Harris, who visited the then colony of the Gold Coast" (Oosthuizen 1968, 55). Harris preached temperance, repentance, baptism, and the rejection of any form of idolatry. He taught belief in one God and "our Redeemer Jesus Christ" (Oosthuizen 1968, 56). Because his evangelization took African thought-forms and idiom, Harris's message made a tremendous impact, reinforcing the African indigenous feeling of dependence on God.

In West Africa, the first mass secession occurred in 1901 when the

Anglican priest James Johnson was transferred from his church. His followers protested and this Anglican congregation eventually became known as the African Church of Bethel (Oosthuizen 1968, 52).

In the category of the spirit churches, there are numerous other movements like the two that we have briefly discussed here. Garrick Sokari Baird, a self-styled prophet who called himself the second Elijah, acquired spiritual prominence in this movement and became a faith healer. He healed the sick, denounced all idolatry, and was against Western medicine as well as alcohol (Omoyajowo 1972, 10). Omoyajowo observes that "the emphasis on divine healing is an answer to one of the problems which drives the believer to traditional religion" (Oosthuizen 1968, 52).

In East Africa, Chief J. K. Mugema cofounded a church in 1914 on the basis of his Christian conviction that through faith in Almighty God the sick could be healed. The emergent Bamalaki Church, nevertheless, did not make much headway because civil authorities intervened. This movement was very strong on biblical and doctrinal convictions. Today it goes by the name Society of the One Almighty God.

Parrinder informs us that the African independent churches in East Africa are neither solely spiritual nor solely political; they tend to combine the two ingredients but lack the extremism of both Aladuraism and Ethiopianism. Mabel Ensor's Mengo Gospel Church was not quite a success because it did not strike a healthy balance.[7] Independency in East Africa is peculiar in that even some white people have founded indigenous churches. For example, one was cofounded in 1929 by an Englishman, Dr. Church, and an African, Simeon Nsibambi. The movement was at first "concerned with a more personal spiritual life, beneath the superficiality of much official Christianity, and it challenged European superiority and made room for African leadership" (Parrinder 1969, 155). But it could never really be stable until the questions of race and power had been resolved.

We must also note that in East Africa, the Gikuyu independent churches "were interested in preserving some traditional customs, notably female circumcision, but they were Christian in intention" (Parrinder 1969, 156). Among the Akan Society in Ghana the churches "stress traditional values such as respect for age and obligation toward family members" (Appiah-Kubi 1979, 120–21). Independency in East Africa has taken aspects of African traditional life seriously. In order to strike an indigenous note the concepts of an African theology would need to develop along some of these traditional lines.

In the Congo the most prominent African independent church movement is Kimbanguism.[8] Simon Kimbangu, its founder, had been educated through the Baptist Missionary Society. After a series of visions and dreams, he founded Kimbanguism, having been himself endowed with healing powers and prophetic insights. Besides Kimbangu, there are other African faith healers in central Africa.

Zionism, founded in South Africa by Ignatius Lekhanyane, was carried on by his son, Edward. It spread into what is now Zimbabwe, Botswana, and a few other neighboring states. Transvaal Zionism was transmitted to Zimbabwe by David Masuka and Samuel Mutendi.[9]

According to Edward Lekanyane's Zionism, "faith-healing, baptism by immersion and the speedy return of Christ, are the major emphases" (Oosthuizen 1968, 37). This is the message Masuka and Mutendi imported to Zimbabwe. Eventually, both men became the leaders of their respective groups; both later became autonomous churches.

In no time, the Fort Victoria area became "fertile soil for the emergence of a multitude of 'Zionist', 'Apostolic', and 'Ethiopian' churches" (Hastings 1979,76). Here spirit churches took priority over Ethiopianism in numbers as well as impact upon society. According to Hastings, there has always been a conscious attempt to maintain apostolic succession from the original Zion in Jerusalem, through North America, South Africa, and now Zimbabwe.

It was in 1932 in the Masvingo fertile "religious crescent" that two really powerful independent churches emerged. The Vapostori, the Apostles of Johane Maranke,[10] became numerically the largest independent church in the country. This apostolic church, although it shared a common origin with Zionism, developed its own ecclesiastical character. Membership identity, for example, is crucial, and a particular African awareness distinguishes it from most other churches in Zimbabwe.

Like Johane Maranke, Johane Masowe had a vision and founded a church. "The message he proclaimed was one of withdrawal from all European things—even at first from acquiring Bibles though he had one himself from the start. Bibles, schools, employment, all alike were to be rejected" (Hastings 1979, 77). The community engaged in industrial arts in order to be self-reliant and self-employed. Unfortunately, because of its political inclination, Masowe left what was then Rhodesia and settled at Port Elizabeth in white-ruled South Africa. Today the Masowe church has become what Hastings describes as "the Korsten Basketmakers, a closed and highly industrious religious community of the Shona, the Apostolic Sabbath Church of God" (Hastings 1979, 78). From this experience, African theology can develop a theological understanding of self-reliance.

African independent churches have emerged all over the continent because the mission churches failed to meet Africa's basic spiritual needs. I share the view of other theologians that the indigenous churches must be seen as "essentially religious movements which have provided the much longed for spiritual home for African Christians" (Hastings 1979, 9). Appiah-Kubi's article (1979, 117) supports this view. He argues that "spiritual hunger is the main cause of the emergence of the indigenous African Christian churches, and not political, social, economic, and racial factors" (117–18).

EMPHASIS ON SPIRITUALITY

African theology, as it develops, needs to reckon with the fact that religious beliefs in Africa are strongly spiritually-oriented. There can be no more suitable beginning than African spirituality, and a theology that seeks to be true to the tradition and heritage of the African people must recognize its spiritual roots.

Omoyajowo insists that the manifestation of the Holy Spirit "is one of the fundamental things that distinguish them [independent churches] from other churches" (1972, 11), while Appiah-Kubi points out that spiritual experience is "the pivot of most African religions" (1979, 118). The Aladura in particular, "believe that they are always guided by the inspiration of the Holy Spirit" (Omoyajowo 1972, 11). The inception of their community is often traced back to visions, dreams, or trances. Such spiritual beliefs play a very significant role in decision-making processes in independency. Christian doctrines of the Holy Spirit, God, and Christology, if formulated in African thought-forms and idiom, will enliven the gospel for the people. Barrett suggests that, like the independent churches, African theology must have a spiritual base (1968, 195). Moreover, since the independent churches are "striving for cultural integrity and spiritual autonomy" and a creative response to the breakdown of old forms of African society, they provide for theologians a framework within which to create a viable African theology.

Some African scholars contend that there is a clear correlation between the role of the Holy Spirit in the Bible and the role of the ancestral spirits in African traditional religion (Appiah-Kubi 1979, 120). If that is the case, African theology can find its origins and begin to develop a doctrine of African pneumatology in this framework. In chapter 1, we indicated the importance of ancestrology. In this chapter we have discovered that the independent churches tend to "capitalize" on spirituality and ancestrology (Appiah-Kubi 1979, 120). African theology can draw from these two sources. Perhaps this spiritual fecundity in the independent churches can replace the spiritual sterility that characterizes the older churches in Africa (Omoyajowo 1972, 11). Spontaneity, another quality of the independent churches, is more conducive to the intercessory function of the Holy Spirit than "the cold, frigid, professionally-aired Christianity that is mainly interested in form" (Appiah-Kubi 1979, 118). The African theological understanding of the Holy Spirit may come from articulation of faith healing, interpretation of dreams, and the seeing of visions, all of which are already commonplace in most African independent churches. Mbiti comments that: "emphasis is . . . laid on the place and work of the Holy Spirit, and during worship services people seek to be possessed by him" (Mbiti 1970a, 307). While Omoyajowo finds that:

> In most cases, the founders of independency are people yearning for spiritual satisfaction, seeking and obtaining answers to questions for which there are no solutions in the Western-established churches [1972, 9].

The independent church movement, unlike mission churches that tend to be mechanically controlled, provides a rich background out of which African theology can be developed with a strong spiritual dimension.

The African independent churches could make a smooth transition from spiritual guidance in traditional religion to guidance by the Holy Spirit in their new faith. Omoyajowo notes that "the role of the healer is similar to that of the traditional diviner or babalawo" (1972,10). This continuity further underscores the significance of the independent churches for an African theology; it suggests the possibility of establishing a continuity between biblical theology and African traditional religion.

When African theology reaches a point where it can address the African people on this spiritual level, then it will become effective for the believer. Omoyajowo acknowledges this spiritual dimension of African independency as the single major factor that has "contributed tremendously to their spectacular evangelistic success" (1972, 10). A theology that develops in this framework will have an indigenous religious character in the formulating of both Christian doctrines and liturgies.

THE INDIGENIZATION
OF DOCTRINE AND LITURGIES

I agree with the claim that "the indigenous churches accept the basic doctrines of the church" (Omoyajowo 1972, 10). In fact, I have observed that they strongly believe in the Bible. Appiah-Kubi's study confirms my position: "The Bible is central to their religious and daily life. They have great love for reading the Bible, a love rarely found even in clergy or religious people of other churches" (1979, 119).

If most of these independent churches treasure the Bible this much, what kind of a theology shall we expect to come out of that matrix? Omoyajowo tells us that "their theology . . . is essentially biblical theology" (1972, 10). The next question is, how much will this biblical taste influence African theologians to develop a *biblical* African theology? Perhaps it is still too early for us to be able to answer. What is not questionable is the fact that most African Christian scholars agree that the Bible is indispensable to any Christian theology. Mbiti notes that "any viable theology must and should have a biblical basis, and African theology has begun to develop on this foundation" (1979a, 90).

Whereas some independent churches still lack a coherent and systematic theology, many of them have carefully and innovatively adapted aspects of the Christian faith and practice to their African milieus, although they do not have written theology. With respect to African liturgies, some African independent churches "are characterized by a greater measure of spontaneity and excitability. Their use of indigenous music is an innovation which accounts for many of their evangelistic achievements" (Omoyajowo 1972, 10). For instance, besides translating the hymns into Shona, their native language, the Masowe sing "Holy, holy, holy" to an African tune and beat. Sung in this way, even Western lyrics can touch African hearts. Thus the concern of theologians for a relevant faith finds a ready liturgical ground in the worship style of many of the independent churches. According to Idowu, African liturgy is

> a people's way of approaching God in worship; a means of expressing themselves, especially in a congregational setting, before God and of assuring themselves of communion with Him . . . a means by which a human soul finds a link with the living spirit who is God [1965, 26].

African theologians are discovering that the type of African liturgy defined by Idowu is already common practice among most African independent churches. Obviously a theology based on what is actually happening is preferable to a merely speculative one based on some abstract philosophy.

Indigenized Christian doctrine and liturgies provide excellent material for an African theology. I share Fashole-Luke's view that the African begins to feel at home in a religious context only when liturgy, hymns, ethical rules, and Christian doctrine are truly identifiable as African.

I believe that an indigenized Christianity will be able to transform a people without condemning their cultural identity. The African independent churches, which consciously promote religious practices affirming African humanity, are in a position to accomplish this transformation.

In this chapter we have seen how African scholars are working to develop an African theology in the theological framework of spiritualization and indigenization. These emphases are capable of providing a context for an African theology that can touch the hearts of the people.

In the wake of political independence, the modern African has been concerned about his or her personal and national destiny as well as a proper African identity. If it affirms the latter, African theology will prove to be of great importance to modern independent Africa.

In the next chapter, I will discuss nationalism and the origin of African theology. It will be apparent that the concerns of theology are similar to most concerns of African nationalism. This should not surprise us because both seek to serve the African people.

Chapter 4

African Nationalism

African nationalism is another major source for African theology. The latter's concerns about Africanization and indigenization had been articulated by nationalists and Pan-Africanists decades before the inception of African theology.

In the struggle to set Africa free from foreign political, economic, social, and spiritual domination, a truly African theology can give expression to nationalism. African nationalism is, in fact, one of the forerunners of African theology, especially in its emphasis on culture, human dignity, liberation, and solidarity.

From its inception, African nationalism has been concerned about three major issues: racial equality, political independence, and the preservation of African culture. These are also themes in African theology that are often interpreted in the light of the Scriptures. I will discuss these elements after outlining the historical background of nationalist movements that led to African political independence.

PAN-AFRICAN AND AFRICAN NATIONALISM

The history of Pan-Africanism begins with the contribution of W. E. B. DuBois, a black American who organized the first of the five Pan-African congresses.[1] This is why W. E. B. DuBois has been generally recognized as the father of Pan-Africanism.[2] The first Paris congress was sponsored by the National Association for the Advancement of Colored People (NAACP), in which DuBois had played an important role.[3]

The purpose of these congresses[4] was "not only to give Negroes throughout the world a sense of identity and solidarity but to work for a definite goal . . . self-determination" (Akintoye 1976, 85). As African theologians attempt to formulate theological constructs on Africanization, these nationalist goals and objectives may provide them with a relevant context.

The Negroes' concern to reap the benefits of their participation in the First World War provoked such questions as these among the Africans in diaspora: If other races are reaping the benefits of the war, why not the Negro and Africans? Why are Africans not to be allowed to shape their own political destiny?

From the very beginning, the Pan-Africanists pressed for racial equality and the use of Africa's resources for the benefit of the African people themselves. This demand emerged from the awareness that "Black men everywhere should unite to liberate themselves" (Akintoye 1976, 98). Racial consciousness was a rather spontaneous development both in the New World and on the main continent of Africa. In the New World, the movement reached its peak under such great black leaders as Marcus Garvey[5] and W. E. B. DuBois.

After a few decades, especially after the Second World War, the focus shifted from Pan-Africanism to African nationalism. More and more political activity surrounded the state of Liberia, which was the only independent Negro nation in West Africa. Unfortunately Liberia soon ran into financial difficulties. Along with Liberia's financial problems, Garvey's conviction by the United States government for alleged fraud killed the back-to-Africa movement (July, R. W. 1970, 460).

Nevertheless the North American blacks had kindled a fire which continued to burn on the continent of Africa. The exponents of Pan-Africanism and the African nationalists tirelessly worked together for the betterment of the black race. The significance for African theology of this initial attempt toward solidarity cannot be overemphasized.

In Africa the best champions of Pan-Africanism were also religious men.[6] Among the outstanding figures was Wilmot Blyden[7] of West Africa. Blyden "extolled African culture and urged educated Africans to give up European values and return to their own culture" (Akintoye 1976, 98). He advocated an all-African church without European attachment. Herein lie some of the ideas that might have led to the beginnings of the All Africa Conference of Churches.[8]

Ferkiss contends that African nationalism received much influence from the New World because

the real catalysts of nationalism were the returning students—men who had studied abroad and been accepted as equals in some countries for some purposes, confirming their self-confidence, men who had studied abroad and who have been denied equality in other countries, firing their resentment [1966, 91].

Kwame Nkrumah of Ghana provides a good example. When he returned home, he brought with him particularized views of Pan-Africanism.

There is an obvious link between Pan-Africanism and African nationalism. For instance, when Nkrumah ascended to political heights, he asked George Padmore, a well-known Pan-Africanist, to serve as his political adviser.[9] According to Geiss, Padmore was behind Nkrumah's initiative to call the first All Africa Peoples' Conference, which was held in Accra in December 1958 (1974, 354). This conference is regarded as the sixth Pan-African Congress, and it represented a continuation of the work that was started by W. E. B. DuBois. This series of congresses culminated when African states began to attain their independence one after another. While the Africans in diaspora generally played an advisory role, African nationalists were in the spotlight. More important, the joint efforts of Pan-Africanists and African nationalists eventually resulted in Africa's political independence.[10] Since African nationalism is not identical with Pan-Africanism, it is necessary to define each of them. The two meanings will serve to elucidate the political movements toward African independence.

DEFINITIONS

W. E. B. DuBois's understanding of Pan-Africanism was "the idea of one Africa," "united in experience" and exposed to the impact of other cultures (1965, 7). This understanding has been interpreted in more modern terms to mean "the desire of Africans to pull together for mutual support, for their full liberation, and a more effective voice in the affairs of the world" (Akintoye 1976, 98).

African nationalism has been defined as "the struggle against domination by overseas imperialists." According to this definition,

Africa as a whole is made "the unit of national identification and hence also the unit of political independence" (Ferkiss 1966, 80).

African theology's concepts of nationalism and solidarity need to be developed within this political framework and definition of nationalism. It is apparent from the definition that as a Third World phenomenon, African theology draws on the themes of unity and the solidarity of the downtrodden.

Since the Pan-Africanist and African nationalist ideas seem to express much of what African theology is concerned about, namely, a united African voice, it is apparent that there is common ground between the two. Consequently, it is not surprising that the African church is attempting to develop a theology of reconciliation. Furthermore, it is my opinion that African theology cannot be apolitical if it acknowledges the political history of the continent.

Ferkiss's definition of African nationalism also points to the outright rejection of domination by foreign powers. Within this framework are emerging theological perspectives on liberation, Africanization, and indigenization. The nationalists' demands to have all African leadership arise from the assertion that Africans, like any other people, can manage their own political affairs. In a real sense, the domination by foreign powers in decision-making positions implies that Africans are inferior and incapable of managing either church or state business.

The theological concern about human dignity, brotherhood, and sisterhood of all people of African descent is undermined unless the nationalist stance is interpreted in a theological language that affirms a full African humanity and includes a spiritual dimension.

Furthermore, the question of a moratorium[11] on missionary personnel and foreign aid is being debated in the light of the nationalist demand that Africa has come of age. Continued dependence on foreign powers undermines African human dignity.[12] Where African nationalists give political reasons for Africans to be independent, African theologians find theological reasons for the need for self-reliance.

In fact, the moratorium debate now being raised in the church has been exhausted in the political arena under the banner of freedom. Initially many African states completely Africanized the new governments; later they asked selected white skilled expatriates to return and serve under black governments if they were willing to do so. Even in nations like Zimbabwe, where power was essentially seized through armed struggle, the whites may be asked to serve only if they accept the fact that the black people are in charge.[13] African theology must develop an understanding that makes both the former oppressor and the former victim feel secure enough to share rights and privileges without a feeling of being exploited or oppressed. Such a formulation will pave the way for genuine reconciliation.

It seems to me, however, that there needs to be a period of *total black presence* before whites come back to serve. For a people who have been colonized for over four decades, continued white presence after independence can be psychologically damaging. I believe that temporary black domination serves to restore African morale and a sense of belonging and superiority. Black domination will engender a proper African identity and pride. This is why African nationalism has also been correctly defined as

> the consciousness of belonging to a particular nation, with pride in its cultural heritage (rather than that of any particular ethnic group), together with an articulate demand for the self-government of that nation in place of alien colonial control [Lloyd 1967, 216].

Notable in this and the previous definitions is the emphasis on cultural heritage and self-government as opposed to foreign rule. The emphasis has characterized the rise of both African nationalism and theology.

AFRICAN NATIONALISM AND AFRICAN THEOLOGY

African theology's concern for Africanization can be developed against this political background, which is based on the concern for human dignity and survival. African nationalism has always been concerned with the preservation of the African cultural heritage. Theologically speaking, this means a search for a theology that is relevant to the African cultural belief systems.

The definitions that we have examined recognize the importance of political independence and cultural heritage, and they explain why African theology is developing concepts that tend to reinforce political power and cultural validity. African theology's claim to set the African at liberty to be who God created the African to be is a theological articulation endorsing what has been pointed out by African nationalists in the struggle for political independence on the continent.

African nationalism operates at two levels: (1) local protest against a particular foreign authority on a specific issue such as racial discrimination, and (2) generalized protest over the whole continent or even the entire black world against a common enemy, such as European domination. This double stratum gives a double strand to African theology. Therefore, there is a contextualized African theology based on a particular area—such as black theology of liberation in South Africa—which at the same time contains a general theme of Africanization. The general theme may touch and unite the whole African or black world, but the particular base, being situational, may be relevant only to a certain region for a specific period.

African theology may develop along a pluriform structure as African theologies, the differences depending on the particular social context. Or African theology may be viewed as a unit comprising theological branches. Although they are all facets of the whole, each has its distinct particularity and emphasis. Any claim for the universality of African theology must be based on a series of authentic contextual reflections and truths.

I contend that African nationalism provides a general context within which theology is being done, for the central theme of nationalism gave rise to the spirit of African theology in the 1950s. African nationalism has also provided a framework within which the church in Africa has developed not only structurally but also politically. The All Africa Church Conference is a good example. It is not sheer coincidence that its first meeting in Ibadan was held in 1958, the same year that Nkrumah called a conference of all independent African states (Akintoye 1976, 102). These independent African states

> resolved to give maximum support to other Africans still fighting for the independence of their countries . . . decided to plan a bigger conference at which a united strategy would be worked out for the liberation of all of Africa [Akintoye 1976, 102].

This resulted in the All Africa Peoples' Conference in Accra in 1958. By their next conference, in 1963, these African states had taken their present form as the Organization of African Unity (OAU).

Simultaneously the Ibadan All Africa Church Conference (1958) planned a bigger conference to which all black churches in Africa were invited. This was also held in 1963, at Kampala, the birthplace of the present All Africa Conference of Churches (AACC). The basic strategy of this organization was to develop a distinctive African church identity and theology. Involvement in the political liberation struggle has also been a major theme at the AACC assemblies (AACC 1975).

Any theological developments within the AACC context can really be regarded as emanating from the general spirit of African solidarity, which is also the spirit of African nationalism. This spirit of unity can be traced back to utterances by the African nationalists who declared that unless all African nations are free, the freedom of a few means nothing. Nkrumah said: "Our task is not done and our own safety is not assured until the last vestiges of colonialism have been swept from Africa" (1975, 240). The commitment of the All Africa Conference of Churches to become involved in the liberation of all African people comes directly from this nationalist thought. Any talk about African solidarity comes from the influence of African nationalism. I think it is possible that an African liberation theology with a global perspective can develop within this nationalist framework.

Regarding the doctrine of human dignity and equality, there is an interesting sequence. Following the Scriptures, missionaries in Africa taught the equality of all people before God. Consequently, African nationalists (most of whom are Christians) have demanded the implementation of this Christian doctrine in Africa. Now African theology is developing concepts along similar nationalist lines. Thus an African doctrine of humanity, for example, cannot be developed apart from the African political understanding of full humanity and equality. Julius Nyerere, the President of Tanzania, says the Arusha Declaration "is based on the assumption of human equality, on the belief that it is wrong for one man to dominate or to exploit another" (1968, 92).

It is important to note that Nyerere's socialism draws heavily from an African traditional lifestyle which is pervaded with African religious beliefs. We have already seen in chapter 1 that African theology draws insights from African cosmology. Likewise, African nationalism may be basing its tenets on the same traditional life that directly provides raw material for African theology.

Nyerere believes that "socialism" is an application to economic and social life of the doctrine of human equality (1968, 95). This nationalist theme of human equality or racial equality can be traced back to the Pan-African Congress held in Paris in 1919 under the auspices of the National Association for the Advancement of Colored People (Ferkiss

1966, 85). This understanding provides African theology with a spectrum out of which a clear theological concept of the doctrine of humanity may emerge. What does it mean in the light of the evil of racism and oppression to say that "man was created in the image of God"?

Socialism implies self-reliance, which means that "for our development we have to depend upon ourselves and our own resources" (Nyerere 1968, 95). This nationalist concept could provide a model for the church's policy regarding the sending and receiving of white missionaries and foreign aid.

African theology deals with concepts and issues, most of which have been raised by African nationalists. Its challenge, however, is to formulate theological constructs in order to help not only church leadership but the heads of state as well.

Both Nyerere and Kwame Nkrumah espouse the doctrine of African freedom and unity.[14] Freedom and unity also constituted the theme of the World Council of Churches at its fifth assembly at Nairobi in 1975 (Kennedy 1976). African theological insights and articulation on the subjects of freedom and unity are being expressed in light of the gospel and African political realities.

If African theology is to be relevant to African social and political as well as spiritual needs, it will have to address themes in the political arena. For instance, African theology needs to articulate what it means to say "Jesus Christ frees and unites." Its task is to develop spiritual dimensions in the interpretation of pertinent nationalist-oriented concepts, so that the nationalists can still relate to the issues after they have been given a theological explication. Theological formulations developing within the context of political concepts of freedom and unity will be enriched by a spiritual dimension that is even more potent than bare political force. At present, African nationalists are working hand in hand with African theologians because both parties seem to share the same vision—that of a united, peaceful, dignified, self-reliant Africa. Examples of the embodiment of African nationalism and African theology are Rev. Ndabaningi Sithole and Bishop A. T. Muzorewa,[15] both of the Republic of Zimbabwe. These two clergymen seem to derive theological inspiration from their involvement in nationalism.

More important, it is ironic that most African nationalists are the academic and spiritual products of the church in Africa or former civil servants in the colonial governments. With regard to this relationship, Ferkiss raises an interesting question: Could it be true that "the more advanced was the process of acculturation to the imperialist . . . in a particular African colony, the greater, by and large, the degree of nationalism''? Or can one claim that "the Christian religion was also a source of inspiration for the nationalist movement" (1966, 83)? If both questions are answered in the affirmative, then it is easy to understand and to accept that African nationalism can provide a context and content for the development of a meaningful African theology. To be relevant to nationalist inclinations, the African theology that emerges from here must be itself a sort of protest theology, protesting against domination for the purpose of affirming African humanity and solidarity. African theology must be liberated from those traditional Christian theological concepts that do not have any reference to the African people.

This spirit of protest may also explain the emergence of the All Africa Conference of Churches, an organization that officially was meant to consist of Africans only. Thus we can expect some overlap between the concerns of the All Africa Conference of Churches and those of the All Africa Peoples' Conference, which is now known as the Organization of African Unity (OAU). Generally speaking, it could be argued that the two organizations are complementary, at least ideologically.

SUMMARY

I have attempted to establish several important points here:

1. We have reached the conclusion that Pan-African activities, with a nucleus in the New World, influenced the development of African nationalism considerably. This conclusion is important for the origin of African theology. I personally think that this relationship between the black nationalists in the New World and African nationalists who were studying abroad and who then returned home (to Africa) is sufficient ground to argue that the spirit of African theology is influenced by black nationalism as well as African nationalism. Therefore why should African theology not reckon with black and African political affairs?

2. We have seen that the political issues that concern nationalists also become important theological issues for the African church. A good example is the current theological emphasis on Africanization. This had been a matter of great concern for African nationalists long before

African theology had taken its present form. This implies that African nationalism has more or less set the agenda for African theology.

3. We have also established that religious leaders in Africa and the United States were among the first to catch the vision of Africa's great destiny. But the vision was best articulated in the nationalist arena and not in black and African theological circles. It is in this sense that we understand African theology to be emerging from nationalism.

4. Both African theology and black theology in South Africa have had to contend with the race problem. Since racial tension was one of the earliest concerns of nationalists in the New World and later in Africa, African theology must take a stance on the question of race in Africa.

The issue of race calls for major treatment in African theology because the self-image of the African people has been distorted by Western culture since the initial contacts between blacks and whites. While black theology has made racism a major issue, as J. H. Cone's *A Black Theology of Liberation* (1970)[16] readily demonstrates, African theologians have focused on Africanization. It is not clear why most African theologians tend to shy away from politicizing their theology. In my opinion, both theologies are concerned about restoring the proper image of black humanity, an image that had been grossly distorted by Europeans and white Americans. Such a task cannot be completed without political involvement.

5. In order for an African theology to be relevant to African needs and aspirations, it cannot develop to any satisfactory degree if it ignores the African political world. The two are closely related in that their initial difficulties, concerns, and goals are very similar and the beneficiary is one, the African. The symbiotic relationship of the two is also evidenced by the fact that in many cases the African nationalist is also the African church leader.

6. We have discovered that most African nationalists are products of Christianity. But ironically, Christianity seems to be part of the nationalists' major enemy insofar as Christianity is generally associated with Western imperialism. Therefore, it is extremely important that African theology articulate the concepts of freedom, human equality, and liberation. The nationalist needs to know where the church stands, since the latter has numerous ties with overseas boards and agencies.

It is clear that aspects of African theology have their origin in African nationalism. The former's task is now to formulate theological constructs on issues that gravely concern the latter. The nationalist needs to be convinced that the Christian religion is not the opiate of the people of Africa and does not retain vestiges of colonialism.

Nationalism and the Christian religion tend to be intertwined. Thus we can expect a theological reciprocity between nationalism and African theology and black theology, and between nationalism and the All Africa Conference of Churches. In the next chapter we will discuss the All Africa Conference of Churches, including its political involvement in nationalism and its impact upon the origin of African theology.

Chapter 5

The All Africa Conference
of Churches

The formal inauguration of the All Africa Conference of Churches
(AACC)[1] in 1963 marked the official beginning of African theology.[2]

It was as a result of Kampala that many African theologians and
church leaders felt impelled to work on an African theology (Dickson
and Ellingworth 1971). The same concern was expressed by Mbiti in a
paper he presented two years later, in which he spoke for his theological colleagues in saying that "the church in Africa cannot . . . afford to
remain without a theology when she is confronted with so many theological challenges today" (1968, 332).

In this chapter I will discuss how the AACC provided an official
context for the origin of African theology. The background of the
AACC will be examined, and the theological ramifications scrutinized.
Then I will discuss the rise of the AACC and the items of its agenda that
delineate the directions in which African theology began to develop.
There are five items: (1) the AACC and a theological concept of
freedom, (2) the AACC and the concept of selfhood, (3) the AACC
and the call for a moratorium, (4) the church's self-understanding,
and, finally, (5) the church and African nationalism.

BACKGROUND

The Christian Council of Churches in Nigeria, with some financial
help from the International Missionary Council, sponsored the All

Africa Church Conference that was held at Ibadan in 1958 (AACC 1963, 5). "It was perhaps the most representative gathering of Christian Africans ever" (AACC 1963, 5). The Provisional Committee [3] had planned that the majority of the delegates should be African. The invitations were carefully calculated.[4] Two-thirds of the delegates were black because it was hoped that the AACC would be an organization led by indigenous people for the purpose of dealing with African concerns. The African church had felt a need that neither the World Council of Churches nor the Christian councils could fulfill.

The Need for the AACC

The great need was for African unity. The various churches had not hitherto been as united as was desirable in light of the nationalist spirit of the time. The churches lacked solidarity on African soil. Each had more in common with its "home church" (Euro-American churches) than with neighboring African churches of other denominations.

Thus, what prompted the creation of the AACC was a need for solidarity (AACC 1963, 5). The churches were not necessarily interested in strengthening denominational ties, but African Christian brotherhood and sisterhood. This is why the AACC, by design, has an "all-African" membership. If it were to "play its role as champion, teacher, counselor, and shepherd during these crucial years" (AACC 1963, 7), the AACC had to be an all-black organization. Africa had had enough of foreign domination, and from the outset its very structure conveyed the message of freedom from foreign rule and domination.

The peak of African nationalism preceded the establishing of this African autonomous body (the AACC). Nationalism had demonstrated that if Africans would only pull their political power and their human and financial resources together, they would become much more vocal and powerful. Thus, the AACC, living symbol of African unity in Christ, encouraged cultural unity, and when it became involved in African political affairs, it also acquired some political status and power.

Theological Implications

There are several obvious theological implications in the formation and existence of the AACC. Most significant of all is the African churches' realization that the important thing in the faith is not one's denomination; rather, it is faith in one Lord. Consequently, an emergent African theology should interpret what Christ is doing, rather than what the Methodists or the Lutherans are doing in Africa. The catholicity of the church began to take on an African meaning. No longer did Rome or New York have the final word on every African church matter. The church trusts that the Holy Spirit who inspires the pope can also inspire the African church through its own cultural medium as well as through the Scriptures.

The churches have found that ecumenicity is more practical than isolationism. For African believers the most important thing is to be Christian; denominations are merely the result of differences in the interpretation and expression of the faith.

By forming a united body, the African churches have prepared themselves to be a "church with a theology." They will pool their resources and construct theological formulations that will give African church leaders a common sense of direction. In fact, the AACC has already accomplished some of its expectations relative to political involvement. The AACC has enough "political muscle" to facilitate and interpret reconciliation among warring African independent states and to assist the oppressed African peoples in their struggle for freedom. Indeed, it is difficult to say which body has a more powerful voice, the more political OAU or the AACC. Suffice it to say that the conference has become a political power to contend with, not only in African politics, but in world matters as well. The World Council of Churches can no longer speak for the church in Africa without consulting the AACC. It has become the mouthpiece through which African churches express their views. Such was the hope and intention of the Ibadan conference.

Preparation for the First AACC

At Ibadan was "laid a foundation which, five years later, would develop into the All Africa Conference of Churches" (AACC 1963, 5). According to the AACC secretary-general's report, "Ibadan was a symbol of the deep stirrings in the hearts of many people in Africa" (AACC 1970, 84). As the secretary-general put it:

The ferment was not only political; within the churches there were deep stirrings as well. The long years of missionary leadership had helped not only to establish the churches in the various countries in Africa, but also to produce indigenous leaders [AACC 1970, 84].

Mostly African leaders attended this Ibadan conference. "For the delegates who came to Ibadan, it was soon clear that Ibadan could only be a beginning and not an end in itself" (AACC 1963, 6). The Ibadan conference made a resolution naming a committee with the express purpose

> to consult with the Christian Councils of Africa, church bodies and other agencies concerned with the witness of Christ in Africa, in order to give consideration to the implementation of the report of this conference and particularly, as to the appointment of a continuation committee and/or a regional secretary [Dickson and Ellingworth 1971, 6].

The faithfulness of the committee members made it possible for the resolutions to materialize.

In preparation for Kampala, consultations and miniconferences were held in many places, covering a variety of subjects. For instance, a miniconference on Christian family life was held in Mindolo Ecumenical Center, Zambia, in March 1963. Another conference on Christian education met at the University College in Harare, Zimbabwe, in 1963. Reports from such conferences would provide African theologians with some of the materials needed for their task of constructing an African theology.

The AACC's program was planned in such a way that it would cover five major areas of concern: (1) the selfhood of the church in Africa; (2) the *Church* and the churches; (3) Christian concerns in the community; (4) economic development and Christian responsibility; and (5) a theology of nationalism (AACC 1963, 11). Discussions of these topics would assist in the beginning of African theology, a theology which "must evolve spontaneously as the church teaches and lives her faith, and in response to the extremely complex situation in Africa" (Baeta 1968, 332). The environment itself was conducive to the search for an African theology. The AACC presented the African theologians with challenging opportunities for the doing of an African theology. What remains is meeting the theological needs that were expressed at the assemblies.

The pertinent challenges would be highlighted at the AACC's assemblies. For instance, *The Drumbeats from Kampala*, which is a record of the events prior to, and at, Kampala, states the challenges that confront the African church. The next assembly was held at Abidjan. *Engagement: Abidjan 1969* is a record and interpretation of the activities of the AACC at Abidjan, as well as a follow-up of some of the resolutions made at Kampala. The events of the third AACC assembly, held in 1974 at Lusaka, are recorded in *The Struggle Continues*. Articles that are especially important for us demonstrate how African theologians are developing theological ideas conceived and hinted at by the AACC at its assemblies. AACC's fourth assembly was held in August 1981 at Nairobi, Kenya.

THE AACC'S CONCEPT OF FREEDOM

The timing of the inauguration of the AACC in 1963 placed the church in the midst of the "independence era."[5] It is out of this sociopolitical milieu that African theology has begun to emerge. The choice of the theme of freedom at the assembly was most appropriate.

African theology is developing a biblically based concept of freedom within the context of African political reality. At Kampala, the chief speakers who delivered papers on freedom in the African church based much of their presentation on biblical theology.

The expectation of the AACC is that African theology will be a biblical theology because most Christian scholars in Africa recognize that "the Bible is the primary and basic source for the development of African Christian theologies" (Fashole-Luke 1975, 263). The AACC, moreover, seeks a theology that is relevant to the African existential situation (AACC 1963, 17). African theology should, therefore, draw theological concepts from both the Old and New Testaments, as well as from African traditional religion. Furthermore, the AACC seems to understand that both Testaments teach that freedom supersedes political liberation. The spiritual and psychological dimensions of freedom need to be explored in order to give spiritual depth to the nationalist concept of freedom (AACC 1963, 17). This task sets the tone for the beginning of an African theology that meets the needs of the African people today.

Because they understand that theological concepts must develop along the same lines as biblical theology, some African theologians have made literary contributions to *Biblical Revelation and African Beliefs* (Dickson and Ellingworth 1971), a book sponsored by the AACC to encourage and demonstrate an African biblical theology. The first consultation of African theologians, which eventually produced *Biblical Revelation and African Beliefs*, had intended to produce an African theological treatise

> by finding an answer to the delicate question of whether there is any correlation between the biblical concept of God and the African concept of God, between what God has done and is doing according to the biblical record and teaching and what God has done and is doing in Africa according to African traditional beliefs [Dickson and Ellingworth 1971, 16].

By following this method of theologizing, African theology encompasses the tension between biblical theology and a theology of African traditional religion.

Whether this book is a successful work on African theology or not is not for me to say here.[6] The point to note is that, since the first AACC assembly in Kampala, African theologians have committed themselves to the task of creating an African theology. This is why I see in Kampala the beginning of serious African theological writing.[7]

THE AACC'S DEFINITION
OF AFRICAN THEOLOGY

It has not been easy to produce a definition of African theology. Aylward Shorter notes that "the first general Assembly of the All Africa Conference of Churches at Kampala in 1963 was ultracautious" (1977, 23) about an African theology that comes out of traditional African culture. Although the concern for an African theology was evident, the issues were not clear enough then to make a definitive statement. Idowu only hints at the definition when he says that for the African Christian "knowledge of God is not totally discontinuous with our people's previous traditional knowledge of Him" (Dickson and Ellingworth 1971, 16).

Since Kampala, African scholars have been motivated to engage in reflective theological exercises on issues lifted up at the first assembly. Since the Kampala mandate, the major sources used in doing African theology are the Bible and African traditional religion.[8] The implication here is that the real concern of the AACC is to establish a way to indigenize the Christian faith and Christianize certain African traditional religious beliefs with the hope of discovering something uniquely relevant to Africans. Thus the AACC works toward a definite African identity.

THE AACC'S CONCEPT OF SELFHOOD

The church's concern for its selfhood[9] provides a further point of origin of African theology. *The Drumbeats from Kampala* reports that for a long time Christianity in Africa has been "foreign" to the African people because it has been presented in Western categories (AACC 1963, 35). The desire, since Kampala, to indigenize Christianity was made concrete by Idowu's book, which was published soon after the first assembly (Idowu 1965). Most African theologians and church leaders agree with Fashole-Luke that it is high time Africans produced "indigenous theologies, which will satisfy the deepest emotional and spiritual needs of Africans" (1975). He is echoing what Idowu had said ten years earlier, yet the point needed to be reiterated.

The report from the second assembly of AACC states:

As churches we assert that our point of departure is and must be the search for a common theological expression which allows us all, denominations, confessions, independent churches, to proclaim a clear and intelligible message [AACC 1970, 114].

The third assembly located African selfhood in the theology of the Incarnation (AACC 1975, 33). To say that humanity is created in God's image means that the former could be complete and autonomous. It also implies that African humanity is capable of foresight and self-determination. At the same time, it is understood as "being-in-relation." The African church is likewise understood as a corporate personality (1 Cor. 12:1–8).

The church's guiding norm is Jesus Christ, who is its head. Lusaka's understanding of the African church's selfhood is clear.

To attain selfhood, it must be a Church which is keenly aware of the direct headship of Jesus Christ; it must also be continually receiving inspiration and guidance directly from Him, through the Holy Spirit [AACC 1975, 34].

In founding the AACC, the African church took the first step in establishing its selfhood. In defining and discussing the concerns of that body, the church finds itself formulating a theology of selfhood and an understanding of its authenticity and universality. Such a theology will shed proper light on highly controversial issues such as the moratorium on foreign funds and missionaries.

The closest the Ibadan theological consultation came to defining African theology was expressed in Idowu's introductory statement:

> Neither theology nor evangelism can be defined in terms of what "we" think "we" want to teach and say to people. They are properly defined in terms of what God has done, what God is doing, and what God is saying to each people in their own native context [Dickson and Ellingworth 1971, 11].

African theology is an articulation of how the church hears God's word and perceives God's acts in the African social context.

Abidjan went a step further than Kampala and offered a tentative definition of African theology. However, the participants caution us: "Since African theology is still in its early stages of development, it is impossible to offer an exhaustive definition now" (AACC 1970, 114). For now:

> by African theology we mean a theology which is based on the Biblical Faith and speaks to the African "soul" (or is relevant to Africa). It is expressed in categories of thought which arise out of the philosophy of the African people [AACC 1970, 114].

Thus African theology is defined as a biblical theology expressed in indigenous categories. Abidjan underscores the emphasis on *Christian* rather than *African* (AACC 1970, 115), yet the emphases belong together. In fact, the correlation of these two elements is the challenge African theology must face.

Although this definition is offered on a tentative basis, it provides a skeleton for an African theology. The least it does is to indicate the important ingredients, namely the Scriptures and the African culture (soul) and worldview (philosophy).

Since the AACC is the framework in which African theology originated and developed, we note the principles it suggested as guides. There are six: (1) "Christ must be at the center of this theology"; (2) a thorough "knowledge of African culture is necessary" in order to relate the faith in the most meaningful manner possible; (3) a combination of these two may result in a powerful and authentic African liturgy; (4) African theology must dialogue with African socialism, capitalism, humanism, and communism—we are cautioned, however, not to make African theology syncretistic in the process of trying to relate Christianity to African traditional beliefs. The AACC acknowledges that the doing of an African theology is not confined to the mission churches; (5) dialogue with the African independent churches should be maintained, and it is recommended also that the curricula of African universities and theological colleges should try to reflect the current concern for African theological thinking; (6) the AACC should encourage Pan-African theological consultations,[10] including black American theologians and what they "are now producing as they try to seek their own identity as black people" (AACC 1970, 115–16).

These guidelines define the course for African theology to follow as it develops not only in the AACC context but in universities, colleges, and other institutions of learning (Mbiti 1970a, 341–42).

The AACC expressed the concern that in order to achieve selfhood, "the church must have a clear theology and a true sense of worship" (AACC 1963, 32). The definition and the guidelines suggested above tend to focus on two basic concerns: the indigenization of liturgies in African churches, and the Africanization of Christian doctrinal formulations for use in the African church. Once these tasks have been accomplished, the church in Africa will have a selfhood and an identity. For this to happen, the African church should be allowed to be on its own for some time, without missionary financial help and personnel.

THE AACC AND THE MORATORIUM ISSUE

The call for a moratorium [11] on foreign white missionaries and foreign funds has led to a new definition of mission at home and abroad. The AACC leadership raised the moratorium question because it felt that as long as missionaries and foreign funds were sent to Africa, the level of stewardship and the sense of African identity among those in positions of leadership would remain low. The moratorium did not arise from hostility; rather it came from a sense of responsibility.

Our focus here is on the issues in the debate on the moratorium as they relate to the origin and development of African theology. The major issues in the debate center on two matters: (1) the question of the theological validity of the claim by the AACC that, in order for the African church to find itself, expatriates and their material support must first withdraw, and (2) the question of power or control and decision making. All other issues in the debate seem to emanate from these two. It is from theological and political perspectives that answers are sought to such questions as: How did the moratorium become an issue for the AACC? Why can the conference not simply implement its convictions?

The Rise of the Call for a Moratorium

Canon Burgess Carr dates the beginning of the modern call for a moratorium to 1961, when the International Missionary Council became integrated into the World Council of Churches at the New Delhi assembly. Later, at the Mexico assembly, the concept was most clearly articulated in the assembly's theme: "Mission on All Six Continents."[12] The significance of this theme was in the awareness that mission work must be reciprocal and mutual, not one-sided. Every continent has needs and other nations can help to meet them if there is a spirit of mutual Christian responsibility. Every continent needs, moreover, to be concerned about its local ministry as well as its ministry abroad. Carr expresses this point very succinctly:

> Even in the missionary-sending lands there emerged a number of *causes* that sensitized the conscience of Christians and underscored the urgency of their missionary calling at home in real and concrete terms [Carr 1974, 37].

Several pressures have led to the idea of a moratorium. First, "the new thinking about the mission of the church" (Carr 1974, 39) has brought about a new definition of mission. There is only one mission of the church to all humanity (Luke 24:46-49), and Jesus Christ is at the head. (All "missionaries" from all six continents receive orders and instructions from Christ, the Head of the Church.)

Second, there is a need for fresh reformulations of language, structures, and patterns so that they adequately express the new understanding of mission. Third, African Christians have become aware of the political and socioeconomic dynamics that exist abroad, yet affect the life of the church at home. They have become conscious of the importance of having their own leaders make decisions for their church.

In view of these three factors, it cannot be said that a call for a moratorium is a new idea that emerged at the AACC assembly at Lusaka and had only a few exponents, such as Canon Burgess Carr and John Gatu. These African theologians were expressing the feeling among many African churches that it was about time the African Christians took full control of their ecclesiastical activities and responsibilities. It was time the African church depended on its own personnel and material resources.

At a mission festival in Milwaukee, John Gatu expressed the call for a moratorium in such a way that the missionary-sending agents and nations were startled. His message "signalled the end of the modern missionary movement as traditionally understood in Africa."[13] However, the call for a moratorium was brought to the African church's fullest attention by Canon Burgess Carr at the third AACC assembly at Lusaka in 1974.[14] Since Lusaka, the issues on the moratorium have roused interesting debates, with the pendulum swinging between theology and politics.

The Theology of the Moratorium

Since there is a theology of mission, it is reasonable to infer that there must also be a theological basis for the call for a moratorium on foreign missionaries and foreign aid. The theological issues of the moratorium have caused much debate, not just between Africans and white missionaries, but also among Africans and among Europeans and North Americans themselves. The subtleties in the debate are not easy to disentangle.

As I see it, there are four issues related to the moratorium. They have to do with the meaning of catholicity, fellowship, liberation, and authenticity. Other implications can be added to these, but here I will discuss only these four in order to make clear the theological issues involved.

Regarding catholicity, the commonest view held by the opponents of the call for a moratorium is that without a white missionary presence, the church in Africa will lose its universality (*AACC Bulletin*, 21). Implicit in this statement is the thinking that the African church, without white missionaries, loses the essence of Christianity. Since the white missionaries brought the gospel to Africa, their presence ensures authentic Christianity. There are some African Christians and white missionaries who cannot conceive of a genuine Christian church in Africa without some white missionaries in it.

But this view is challenged. Burgess Carr poses the question: "Is it really true that the catholicity of the church is linked to the presence of missionary personnel?" (Carr 1975). For most African theologians, the answer is in the negative. Rather, it is the presence of the Holy Spirit that authenticates the community of believers, whether in Europe, America, Asia, or Africa. To require the presence of white Christians as a condition for the Holy Spirit is to affirm and confirm the allegation that Christianity is a white people's religion. African theologians contend that the African believer can receive and be guided by the Holy Spirit. (Chapter 3 has demonstrated the indispensable role of the Holy Spirit in the African church.) My own opinion is that catholicity is not invoked by a multiplicity of races, but is ensured by the presence of the same Christ, the Lord, in every land. In fact, to claim that unless whites are present in the African church there can be no catholicity is a narrow, materialist view. Those who favor the moratorium are rejecting the implication that the essence of the church is "refrigerated" in Rome, New York, London, or Paris. They are claiming the presence of Christ everywhere, certainly wherever his church exists. This is the true meaning of catholicity.

Exponents of the moratorium are accused of racism when they ask the white missionaries to return or stay at home with their funds. The African church is charged with being isolationist, rejecting and contradicting the spirit of fellowship that ought to characterize the church of Jesus Christ everywhere. The church is also accused of being divisive along racial lines.

The response from those who call for a moratorium is simple. Who brought Christianity to Africa in its denominational compartments? Who sends money to Africa tied with strings that say "for United

Methodists only" or "for Presbyterian High School lab expenses only"? Can a United Methodist-supported medical doctor serve in an indigenous African Christian Church in Zaire? No! Burgess Carr is right. Isolationism "is maintained and perpetuated by those same financial and personnel policies, agenda-setting and decision-making processes that have given rise to a call for moratorium" (Carr 1975, 25).

The point is clear. Through the AACC, the African churches are prepared to put their resources together to feed the refugees. But if the overseas decision makers had their way, they would want their mission churches in Africa to maintain and emphasize denominationalism. The theological ramifications of this denominationalist tendency are devastating. The missionary-sending agents serve people only if the former are assured of the credit and the glory. This type of church has definitely lost its image as "the Body of Christ"; such a church expresses isolationism rather than universality and fellowship.

More important, the exponents of the moratorium advocate a chance to establish a deeper commitment to Christ and the mission of the church. True fellowship can exist only among liberated people who share the faith from the point of view of equality, not inferiority versus superiority. Indeed, one of the stated goals of the moratorium is that it aims to produce African churches "whose relationships with other churches are based upon *equality* under the lordship of Jesus Christ" (*AACC Bulletin*, 28).

The theme of liberation is specifically lifted up in the theological discussion of the call for a moratorium. As long as decisions for the African mission churches are made in New York, Paris, or London by executive members of the respective boards and agents (some of whom have never been to Africa, or only to Zimbabwe as tourists), African needs and aspirations may be overridden. Thus, a handful of Euro-American policy makers dominate thousands upon thousands of African Christians who are said not to know what is good for them. For such oppressed masses, moratorium means liberation (*AACC Bulletin*, 26).

Having been liberated to be their real selves, the African Christians can experience an authentic faith and live up to their Christian responsibilities. Moratorium means authenticity of the faith, and makes possible liberation of the African churches from a feeble state to a responsible state.

The reason most of the African independent churches are thought to be an authentic expression of the Christian faith is that they are independent of the subtle domination, restrictions, and limitations of the dominant churches in Euro-America. More important, they are biblical. In addition to the theological reasons for a moratorium—catholicity, fellowship, liberation, and authenticity—African theologians find biblical backing in the missionary activities of St. Paul. There is no need to catalogue them here.

Finding no theological reasons to explain why white missionaries find it offensive when the African Christians say: "Leave us alone for a while, so that we may be able to discover ourselves, and you, in Jesus Christ" (*AACC Bulletin*, 28), the theologians conclude that it must be a matter of political power and control.

Political Implications of the Moratorium

Though there is nothing wrong with receiving funds and services from a neighbor, if the services and funds are used to incapacitate human spiritual growth there is a theological difficulty. The missionary-sending boards and agents spiritually cripple the African church leaders by treating them as perpetual juniors. The Africans cannot be entrusted with funds from abroad; they are thought to be incapable of making responsible decisions. It is alleged, besides, that they do not really know what is good for themselves.[15]

African Christians who conceptualized the moratorium had come to a point where they would rather do without half their necessities than be flooded with materialism and lose their African human dignity. The Africans who urge the call for a moratorium are prepared to face the consequences of "biting the hand that feeds them"—the same hand that is also strangling them. It is not an easy decision! Far from being a luxury, this moratorium is a very painful option.

I think the missionary-sending boards and agents are persisting because they are enjoying some prestige at the expense of African church people. African church leaders who oppose the call for a moratorium are only confirming the prophetic role of the call itself. Their refusal to be self-reliant demonstrates the serious need for salvation of the whole person. I contend that continued support from overseas contradicts Christ's promise that we have life and have it abundantly, because unless there is a moratorium, the Africans will remain perpetual recipients of the abundance of Christians overseas.

Africans who oppose the moratorium argue that they need time to become financially independent, as well as time to train indigenous personnel. The difficulty with this position is that they put themselves into a vicious circle. The decision makers, who are rarely African, determine the policy of the church. Unless they decide to train indigenous leaders there cannot be any. Until the denominational executives are prepared to relinquish their comfortable posts, no Africans can rise to those heights. The key principle to remember is that unless the oppressed struggle to liberate themselves, their oppressors will not do it for them. The Shona say *mwana asingachemi anofira mumbereko,* "unless the child on the mother's back cries, there is no way the mother can tell that it is uncomfortable."

The moratorium call is a call for self-reliance. The AACC has provided the African churches with a way of finding themselves and establishing a self-understanding so that they can reach maturity.

THE CHURCH'S SELF-UNDERSTANDING

The origins of African theology may be traced to the awakening of the church to its need to understand itself. The AACC had the privilege of being the first comprehensive Christian body in Africa to pose the question: What is the church? The answer lends itself to a theological discourse that is African because it is an African question. It is raised by Africans in their own socioreligious context and the response is by African theologians.

Kampala and Abidjan understand the church to be "a manifestation of the life of Jesus Christ of which the church is the body" (AACC 1963, 37). This definition is biblical.[16] Kampala also expressed the belief that "the church draws its life from the Word of God." Therefore, "it is . . . possible to have an African manifestation of the life of Christ" (AACC 1963, 37). African ecclesiology comes out of these understandings.

To accomplish its objective,

the Church in Africa must have an adequate and clear theology. Also, the Church in Africa must develop her own liturgies which are to grow out of the devotional experience of the Church, and are to take into account, as well, the cultural and cultic background of the people [AACC 1963, 38].

Both God, who is revealed through traditional beliefs, and Jesus Christ, who is known through the Scriptures, can be understood meaningfully by Africans only when approached through their traditional background of worship and liturgies. Similarly, African theological insights into the idea of the church gain depth through the African traditional understanding of God, who is the life of the church.

The relation of the church to the world community is crucial. If the church is the manifestation of the Body of Christ, then it "must cease presenting itself as a society formed of men and women preparing themselves for heaven after death or wishing to be considered by the world as a 'society of puritans' " (AACC 1963, 38). The AACC encourages sociopolitical involvement for the purpose of helping the oppressed liberate themselves. African theology, as it develops, must look into present realities, addressing them in terms of the godly life and dealing with them in ways that manifest Christ. The AACC's understanding is that

> the Church is a community of men and women restored, through Jesus Christ, to fellowship with God, sinners living by pardon and the grace of God. Such a community can only be open to the world and turned towards it [AACC 1963, 38].

This concept of the church inevitably leads to sociopolitical involvement. An African theology that would satisfactorily meet the needs of such a church would have to draw its raw materials from the social sciences in addition to the Scriptures, traditional religious beliefs, and the independent church movements. The African understands life holistically.

African theology must be based on the church's self-understanding that it has a mission to the world in which it finds itself. While the missionaries put much theological emphasis on saving individuals from hell for heaven, the African concept of the church emphasizes salvation from pietistic isolationism, for the purpose of selfless social involvement. "The mission of the Church in relation to the world is the point of departure of all other ministries" (AACC 1963, 39). AACC intends to eradicate the colonial mentality by developing a spiritual concept of liberation that frees the whole person. It follows that African theology must employ a holistic approach in formulating and articulating its theological constructs.

The church asks: "If the Christian refrains from engaging in . . . increasing struggle toward a better existence and a greater liberty, who will engage in it?" (AACC 1963, 58). A theology that will help to make this world a better place is a theology of involvement in all aspects of African life, and of obedience to God's word. If the church is on God's side, there should be nothing to fear.

Christ was not afraid to contaminate Himself in the eyes of his contemporaries by eating with tax-collectors, free women and others considered to be in a permanent state of sin by the Jewish doctors [AACC 1963, 58].

He associated with them in order to save them.

An African theology that understands the church to be "the Body of Christ" will seek to lead the church to act in a Christlike manner. In short, a theology of involvement is consistent with Christ's principles. The church maintains that nationalism "must aim at the establishment of freedom and justice and the respect of human dignity" (AACC 1963, 60). Nationalism should be an instrument of peace and "international solidarity," not a means to dominate other nations. Secular involvement and power should be, for the church, a way of establishing and maintaining a wholesome humanity.

Since Kampala, the church in Africa has been designated as a guard, at the same time that it is involved in national affairs. The AACC contends that the church should maintain a prophetic role and insist on truth, justice, and peace. It must resist all forms of oppression, discrimination, injustice, and corruption. Nevertheless, the church as "guard" does not stand aloof. In crises, it must play an active role. Where political leaders, parties, governments, and power blocs are in conflict, the church must step in to bring about the "reconciliation which is in Jesus Christ" (AACC 1963, 62).

THE IMPORTANCE OF THE AACC FOR AFRICAN THEOLOGY

The AACC is an important source for African theology because its influence is broad, and it has provided definite norms to be followed. Further, the AACC is significant for theology because it deals with crucial concepts such as African nationalism in such a way that freedom acquires a spiritual dimension. I believe this is what Christ means when he says, "I have come to fulfill," not to condemn.

A major contribution of the conference is to make available necessary raw materials of theology, drawn from those who confess Jesus as Lord and Savior. It is, moreover, a testing ground for African theological concepts—an especially important function because there is no guarantee that all African churches will accept any given theology. The AACC's purpose is to provide the churches with a united voice. AACC may also be the only major Christian body vocal enough to publicize an African theology, and let the world know what the African theologians are thinking. The AACC maintains a "theology desk" at its Nairobi headquarters, to assist churches in theological understanding of controversial issues. At the desk in Nairobi, African theology finds a geographical focal point. Theological articles with new insights are edited and printed there. Also, by hosting theological consultations relating to African concerns, the AACC serves to distinguish relevant matters from irrelevant ones and disseminate information on the former throughout Africa.

Throughout Part I, we have discussed how African cosmology is a proper background for the origin of African theology; we have established that since traditional beliefs are based on a true revelation of God, the African worldview provides the theologian with material for an African theology. We have discussed the importance of African independent churches for the indigenization of Christianity; and finally, we have seen that it is largely through the AACC that African theology has gained firm and meaningful ground on the continent.

Three major types of theology in Africa south of the Sahara have been the result of these influences: (1) African *traditional* theology; (2) African theology, and (3) black theology in South Africa. A discussion of these three constitutes Part II.

PART II

VARIETIES OF THEOLOGIES IN SUB-SAHARAN AFRICA

Chapter 6

The Theology of African Traditional Religion

In discussing the origins and development of African theology, it is appropriate to devote a chapter to African traditional theology. While theologians agree with Mbiti that there is an African tradition and admit that their people have always been notoriously religious (Mbiti 1970a, 1), only a few of them tell us what African *traditional* theology is. They even disagree about the terminology to be used.

A DEBATE ON TERMINOLOGY: SEMANTIC OR SUBSTANTIVE?

In the controversy over the meaning of the term *African theology*,[1] the question is whether it means African *Christian* theology or African *traditional* theology, or a combination of both. It is not clear whether the problem is merely semantic or involves substantive issues.

McVeigh argues that since "those who talk about African theology are by and large Christians who are interested in interpreting the meaning of Jesus Christ for the African worldview" (1974b, 8ff.), there is no need to be pedantic about terminology; the term *African Christian theology* can be used interchangeably with *African theology*. John Mbiti, however, favors the term *African theology,* which is the title of one of his articles (1976b). Fashole-Luke, on the other hand, prefers *African Christian theology,* arguing that there is no Christian theology apart from that which is based on the Bible, and that theology is automatically Christian by virtue of that fact (1975). (With such an argument, one might expect Fashole-Luke to omit the adjective *Christian,* but he does not.)

J. K. Agbeti adds heat to the controversy with his position that African theology is distinct from African Christian theology. The latter, it seems, is *Christian,* whether it has been indigenized or not; the former is *traditional,* whether it has been systematized or not (1972). It follows that a theology of African traditional religion should be quite different from Christian theology, because the latter is based on Jesus Christ, while the former is founded on general revelation. Agbeti (1972) argues that African *traditional* theology is to be distinguished from African *Christian* theology because one is theocentric, the other Christocentric. Other scholars acknowledge a possible distinction between the two but conclude that the difference is not substantive.

It might be argued that African theology is not the same as African Christian theology. The former may be seen as placing its emphasis on the traditional thought of African Religions, with the latter stressing Christianity's relationship to traditional thought. In reality, however, these sharp distinctions are not made, and the two tend to be identified [McVeigh 1974b, 9].

My own view is that the problem is not merely semantic. Since African theology is done by Christians for the church and is based on the Bible, it is Christian theology and differs substantively from *traditional* theology in Africa. I shall, in this chapter, use the term *African theology* in that sense. And I shall use the term *African traditional theology* with the understanding that its basis is African traditional religion, not Christianity. This, however, is not the last word on this debate. It is only a temporary solution to the problem, but to seek a definitive solution is not my task here.

There is little doubt that traditional religions in Africa may receive theological interpretations. African traditional theology, although it is not a systematic discipline, has been defined by Agbeti as "the interpretation of the pre-Christian and pre-Moslem African peoples' experience of their God" (1972, 6). While this definition obviously does not adequately cover modern Africans' interpretation of their experience of God outside the Christian context, still, it has value because it suggests that "talk about God" can happen without the aid of the written word (traditional religion in Africa is transmitted orally) or knowledge of Christ. Agbeti is right to point out that the need for a distinctive study of African religious concepts, without confusing them with Christian concepts, cannot be overemphasized.

Moreover, a traditional theology can develop only as traditional religious experience is reflectively and critically interpreted in a systematic way (Agbeti 1972, 7). John S. Mbiti's *Concepts of God in Africa* is a rare attempt to do this. Mbiti's method is less reflective than descriptive and thus brings African traditional theology close to biblical theology with its descriptive nature. And his book does justice to traditional theology by refraining from any reference to Christ.

Though there is a sharp distinction between African *traditional* theology and *Christian* theology, they share one vital element—a "living faith in God" (Agbeti 1972, 7). In this sense, African traditional theology is sometimes thought of as a *preparatio evangelica* (Dickson and Ellingworth 1971, 180). Traditional religion is not a dead religion. It is still practiced in Africa today. When we speak of "a living faith in God," we need to bear in mind that most of its sources are living memories, handed down from generation to generation. To call this living religion "traditional" in no way relegates it to the past.

SOURCES

An oral tradition—the concepts of African traditional religion being passed on from one generation to another—means that Africans receive religious ideas through cultural and linguistic structures, such as prayers, proverbs, myths, art, experience, and various religious symbols and rituals. These are the sources of African traditional theology.

Prayers

The most obvious source is traditional prayers. One reads:[2]

> God! give us health
> God! give us raided cattle
> God! give us the offspring
> Of men and cattle [Mbiti 1975b, 71].

This prayer is only one of numerous standard prayers that portray God as Almighty, the giver of all good things in life (Agbeti 1972, 7).

Another example is the prayer of the people of Ghana: *Asase trew, na Onyame ne panyin,* "The world is wide, but God is the Master" (Agbeti 1972, 7), which places God at the apex of creation. What is more, as Master, God is believed to be in control of the entire universe, including both spiritual and physical forces. African people have experienced God as the Almighty, generation after generation; time has shown them that God is Master over all. In a cattle raid, success is made possible by God because God understands their need to survive.

The African traditionalist believes that, through prayer, God's promise will eventually materialize. God is understood to be a reality whose benefits are tangible and are intended to meet human need in concrete ways. Africa's God is not just a philosophical concept. God is real, even though one cannot see God (Sawyerr 1970, 10). Mbiti writes: "God . . . emerges as the clearest and most concrete spiritual reality" (1975b, 4).

Prayer is the means by which Africans can communicate their survival needs to God, the Great Provider. To understand God's ways and dealings, one looks into the traditional "wisdom literature."

Proverbs

In the absence of the written word, Africans have depended on "myths, proverbs, invocations, prayers, incantations, rituals, songs, and dreams" (Pobee 1979, 21) to preserve knowledge over the years. "African peoples record their great ideas and serious reflections in proverbs" (Lugira n.d., 57). These words, now beginning to be written down, contain and convey African wisdom and theology. Before they can constitute *theology* according to the Christian use of the term, however, they must be collated regionally and interpreted systematically. A link between the two theologies is found in the Bible's use of proverbs and, we might add, myths, prayers, and experiences as well.

Lugira makes a crucial point when he identifies the proverbs as a theological source:

A proverb in African tradition is not only a didactical saying, it is a storehouse of native wisdom and philosophy. A proverb on God is seriously a talk, a reflection on God the unravelling of which may result in books. It is African theology [n.d., 57].

I am aware that not all scholars accept the notion that African prayers and proverbs are loaded with theological insights. All the same, there is a good number who understand that "it is abundantly clear that Africans, apart from being imbued with the sense of religion, have also, from time immemorial, had a theology in their own way" (Lugira, n.d., 57).

Mbiti is one of those who argue that proverbs are a source of traditional theology. He informs us that various ones are used to express the idea of God as the sustainer of life: "Sustenance is exercised through a mysterious, inaudible, and invisible power of God" (Mbiti 1970b, 35). For example, some African tribes hold that "the life of an old man is sustained by God, and his death is caused by God calling him away" (Mbiti 1970b, 35).

A belief common among African peoples is that God is not only the sustainer, but also the author of life. "God gives and God takes away."[3] Apart from proverbs, there are in Africa numerous oral collections of myths—stories that express mysterious phenomena and help people understand the mysteries of birth, life, and death.

Myths

Mbiti finds that myths "are often the most effective means of keeping ideas circulating from one place to another and from one generation to the next" (1975a, 77). Consequently, much African traditional theology is contained in mythical garb. "Traditional African thinking was mythical. It was bound up with the beginnings of things, with creation and the primeval age" (Sundkler 1960, 100). Myths provide Africans with the best context in which to live out their theology. Myths

constitute an "original revelation," which is re-acted in annually recurrent festivals, in a rhythm which forms the cosmic framework of space and time. The myths span the whole of existence, from heaven to the hut and the heart of the individuals: in fact, from cosmos to clan [Sundkler 1960, 100].

African Experience

The sources we have discussed constitute the substance of African theology. These sources are not just conceived intellectually; they are created during the peoples' experience of the divine in the African social context. For instance, a proverb may be "coined" on the basis of a series of experiences over a long time. When a God-encounter is witnessed by several individuals or even communities over several generations, that experience is "traditionalized" and incorporated into the body of African religious beliefs. The Africans through their personal experience are themselves a very vital source of African traditional theology.[4] I have mentioned earlier that Africans "live out" their theology in traditional ways of living.

CONTENT

When we speak of the sources of African traditional theology a key word is *experience*. Agbeti says: "The African traditional experience of the Supreme Being is . . . practical" (Pobee 1973, 5). This experience, interpreted by Africans, is the essential *content* of African traditional theology.

Reflective thinking is part of African experience. While earlier scholars have placed more emphasis on experience than on reflection, I recommend a balance between the two. The fact is that experience encompasses both praxis and reflection. For instance, "When an illness is diagnosed by a traditionalist as the result of the evil eye of a witch in the family, reflection upon experience of a man in the world has already taken place" (Pobee 1973, 5). In African life that act of faith and theological reflection occurs, even though it may seem very casual. This is the case in the following example:

When a man throws down his first morsel of food, it cannot be a thoughtless waste of food. He reasons that he is buying the goodwill of the numerous hosts of spirits about him, who are able to influence his life for good or for ill [Pobee 1973, 5].

The interpretation of these experiences is theology (Agbeti 1972, 6). The main problem with African traditional theology is that the reflections are not recorded, nor are they systematically formulated. As a result, they tend to be neglected or even lost.

Since we have maintained that experience is essentially the content of African traditional theology, what is its nature? "In the African culture, 'experience' is a way of life" (Mbiti 1979b, 75). Since experience and theology are two sides of the same coin, the African's daily activities could be interpreted as a manifestation of African theology. For example, the act of dropping a morsel of food for the ancestors and other spirits to receive is experiential and theological at the same time. We are immediately cautioned that not all experience is theological. Experience that is theological has some bearing on the God who is worshipped (Mbiti 1979b, 75). Hence, theology is "the interpretation of a people's experience of God, the Supreme Being or the ultimate reality, and his dealings with them in history" (Agbeti 1972, 6).

When the interpretation of African religious experience is given a Christian formulation, African *traditional* theology could become Christian theology. The latter is interpreted in the light of Christ's teachings, the former in the light of what God has revealed to the African religious consciousness. The two are not necessarily exclusive of one another. In each case, it is God who chooses to be revealed, whether through the Son or through a bush[5] without a name.

An Emerging Theological Perspective

To say that African traditional theology is an interpretation of traditional African religious concepts places the former at the level of our everyday experience, since religion permeates all the departments of African life. Theology, like religion, undergirds all of life. It is not meant to be a surprise package.

African theologians do traditional theology descriptively more often than reflectively. In *Concepts of God in Africa* Mbiti provides a good example of a descriptive theology.[6] Nevertheless, John Pobee contends that traditional theology is a reflective theology; it is not just a "danced out" theology (1973, 5ff.).

African traditional theology needs to develop an identifiable *methodology*. But it does not necessarily have to be systematic, if that is alien to African thought-forms. The problem is that most African theologians, even those who are the exponents of African traditional theology, seem to insist that it should be developed systematically.[7] This prescription invites difficulties, and an alien product, since it results from a Western methodology.

African traditional theology does not have to be structured along the same lines as Christian theology for two reasons. First, the structure of traditional theology should be determined by its content, and its content is not the same as that of Christian theology. While the latter is based on Graeco-Roman philosophical presuppositions, traditional theology is essentially African. Second, the structure of African traditional theology is determined by an African cultural *modus operandi*, over against the Western or Eastern method. Africans differ from non-Africans in their culture more than anything else, and one's method of thinking (reflection) is influenced more than anything else by one's culture. What distinguishes Africans' culture from that of others must also make their traditional theology different from theologies *of* and *for* other cultures and religions. When these two criteria are satisfied, it may be possible to construct an African traditional theology that will make a significant contribution to Christendom. If African culture does not formulate its tenets according to a systematic linguistic structure, theologians need not be expected to formulate traditional truths systematically.

I believe that in order for traditional theology to be a genuine African product, it should be faithful to the African way of thinking, which is based on a prescientific cosmology. Only an African epistemology will yield a distinct African traditional theology. From time immemorial, Africans have had their religious ways of knowing. A traditional theologian must first recapture this epistemology[8] before she or he starts doing traditional theology for a prescientific mentality in a postscientific world. An African epistemology is one of the most vital tools necessary for the construction of an African traditional theology.

To call for "sound philosophy" and "systematics" is inviting foreign criteria for the doing of traditional theology. Whether or not these tools are suitable for theology is not my point here. My real concern is that they are foreign to African tradition. Using them may yield a "logical" theology; however, the traditional theologian is not interested in just logic but also in a coherent African traditional theology that is relevant to the African believer.

By rejecting Western systematics, I am not necessarily advocating an "unsystematic" traditional theology. We are not dealing with opposites, but with contexts. My argument is that traditional theology should not be subjected to Western structures and methods, for it is not intended to serve the latter; and the reverse is also true.

If traditional theology is not created by the use of Western tools, what does this imply for doctrines that have been based on Western philosophical presuppositions? New formulations are inevitable. Let us briefly consider two major doctrines: the Trinity and salvation.

The Trinity

The Christian doctrine of the Trinity teaches that the Godhead consists of the Father, the Son, and the Holy Spirit, and that the three persons are simultaneously one. In traditional theology, a composition of the three in one was made, even prior to the historical event of the Incarnation. The Shona believe that God's unity exists in multiplicity.

A form of God's Trinity or Triad is reported among the Shona and Ndebele peoples. In one area of the Shona country, God is conceived of as "Father, Son, and Mother." Among the neighboring Ndebele, there is a similar belief "in a Trinity of spirits, the Father, the Mother, and the Son" [Mbiti 1970b, 30].

But the important point for the Shona is not the multiplicity of God, but what God does in these varying modes of being.

First, it helps to substantiate the fact that God chooses who will witness God's self-revelation and what form that revelation will take. If God was revealed to the Shona even before the Incarnation, could we then say that Africans knew Christ in an African way long before Jesus of Nazareth? What is the importance of the historical Jesus for African traditional theology if we concede that African theology already knew of him in pre-Christian ages? This leads to the concept of the preexistent Christ.[9] African traditional theology can shed light on this idea.

The significance of the African concept of a trinitarian God prior to Christianity is that it renders the traditional African culture "Christian" in a peculiar sense. Defined in this new way, a "Christian" religion could emerge from the African culture in an indigenous form. The work of Christ in Africa would have to be rediscovered. The *meaning* of the Incarnation, rather than its history, would then become the essence of Christianity.

Salvation

Another traditional Christian concept that will need reinterpretation is the doctrine of salvation. If we concede that the African Trinity implies the presence of Christ within the African culture, one may say that salvation is a built-in concept there as well. Since the idea of survival dominates in African culture, I submit that salvation is the African mode of being that makes survival happen. In traditional religious beliefs, any life-saving act is ultimately attributable to God.

Salvation is an African spiritual mechanism that works through any agent, including historical reality, to rescue or save an endangered life. For instance, a man who is washed away by a flood may be thrown on a tree trunk lying across the flooded river. If his life is saved by that log, he can say: "Were it not for that log, I would have perished." He rejoices that he has been saved from physical destruction. Salvation is not only spiritual; in the African context, salvation must be holistic. The African traditional theologian knows that that log has no "intention" to "save" anyone, but God uses that log to physically save a creature. Most Africans who find themselves rescued from this kind of danger would attribute such a salvation to their ancestral spirit. It is through the spirit that one is saved, or rescued, or redeemed; but the total event of salvation is God's plan.

Here again, the important point is that God's self is revealed to the African people in various forms and modes of being. In each case God is working to enhance human survival. God works in the form of a physical reality—the log that saves us. As an invisible spirit, God cares for us. Salvation is an event during which one's survival is accomplished through the intervention of an external power. This is extremely important because it demonstrates that salvation is, by definition, wrought by the external power. The articulation of these forces that enhance life is African traditional theology only if the interpretation is done in the light of God's justice and grace.

In the next chapter, this external power is identified as Jesus Christ, the only power by which we can be saved. We now move into a discussion of African theology, as it is contained in the Scriptures and the Christian tradition.

Chapter 7

African Theology

Since its inception about two decades ago, the theology of the church of Jesus Christ in Africa has been a matter of consuming interest among a number of African scholars. I have referred to many of their works often in my earlier chapters.[1] It is proper that we now trace the progress of their efforts to develop a viable African theology for the church.

With the understanding that this theology is being done by Christians for the church, I shall in this chapter refer to it simply as "African theology," even though other theologians may prefer to call it "African Christian Theology." Both expressions clearly distinguish it from "African *traditional* theology."[2]

THE THEOLOGICAL HERITAGE IN AFRICA

Data on the origin and development of African theology can be drawn from two sources. Edited books and articles that are the product of important theological consultations are one source. Books and articles written by individuals on specific subjects or pursuing a specific study are another. Since I am drawing mainly upon written theology in this work, I shall use both sources: books and articles expressing the opinion of one person and books and collections emanating from an assembly.

Following the first assembly of the All Africa Conference of Churches (AACC) in 1963, a theological consultation was organized in 1966. The purpose of the consultation, which was sponsored by the AACC, was to give African theologians an opportunity to work out a

Christian theology for African churches by drawing from biblical and African traditional beliefs. This consultation became the first organized attempt by African Christian theologians to put together a theological book. The result was *Biblical Revelation and African Beliefs*, edited by K. A. Dickson and Paul Ellingworth, published in 1969. *Biblical Revelation and African Beliefs* is a series of eight essays. Traditional African religious beliefs are given a prominent place in a conscious effort to formulate a theology that would be relevant to the experience of African people. Of the eight chapters, seven discuss traditional concepts of God, sacrifice, and humanity.[3] These discussions relate these and other concepts to biblical ideas, but their chief value is that they move toward a reformulation of Christian doctrines in the African idiom and thought-forms.

In 1971, another significant conference was held in Dar es Salaam.[4] This one was important for African theology, as it discussed the pertinent issues of black identity and solidarity. These themes had been articulated as early as 1919 at the first Pan-African Congress,[5] and they have been reiterated by the All African conferences at Abidjan and Lusaka.

An even more pertinent theological meeting was held at Makerere University in Uganda the following year.[6] E. E. Mshana tells us that the major purpose of this consultation was to legitimate, justify, and define African theology (1972a, 19). It was of particular significance in that it brought theological studies into an academic environment. Today African theology is being done in the universities as well as in the church.

To construct a meaningful African theology, the Makerere consultation resolved that African theologians must turn to the everyday life of the African church. The consensus was that "any theology which is divorced from the church life is not true theology. Church life produces Christian theology" (Mshana 1972a, 19).

These consultations accomplished one of their goals, namely, to stimulate the doing of an African theology. Since these early consultations, interest in African theology has continued to grow, both in the church and in the universities.[7]

In 1976, the Ecumenical Dialogue of Third World Theologians met in Dar es Salaam to discuss Third World theologies.[8] This conference once more provided an atmosphere within which African theology was discussed and defined. But it was the Ghana theological consultation in

1977 that actually focused on African theology.⁹ The book that came out of that consultation, in 1979, *African Theology en Route*, edited by Appiah-Kubi and Torres, is the most comprehensive work on African theology at the time of this writing.

Besides the books that resulted from consultations, there are works on African theology by individuals. Aylward Shorter's *African Christian Theology* attempts to demonstrate "how African Christian theology must grow out of a dialogue between Christianity and the theologies of African traditional religion" (Shorter 1977). *Toward an African Theology* by John S. Pobee emphasizes translating Christianity into genuine African categories in order to make the designation "African theology" meaningful.¹⁰

There is a plethora of articles by various African theologians. The ones that are most relevant to and influential for our study are: E.W. Fashole-Luke's "The Quest for an African Christian Theology" (1975), M. J. McVeigh's "Sources for an African Christian Theology" (1974b), and Harry Sawyerr's "What is African Theology?" (1971b). John Mbiti has been the most prolific contributor on African theology.¹¹ Most notable is his "African Theology" (1973a). Appiah-Kubi's "Why African Theology?" (1974) strongly rejects the notion of prefabricated theologies. Desmond Tutu wrote "Black Theology/African Theology—Soul Mates or Antagonists?" (1975). These articles basically make a case for African theology (or African Christian theology, depending on what terminology the authors prefer).

SOURCES

African theology draws theological insights from at least the following sources: (1) African traditional religion; (2) the Bible; (3) African independent churches; and (4) the All Africa Conference of Churches. I will discuss each of these sources and their significance for Christian theology.

African Traditional Religion

It is generally agreed that for Christian theology to be meaningful to African Christians, it must be translated into African traditional categories and thought-forms (Pobee 1979, 17–18). Unless Christianity takes root at the survival level of the believer, African theology cannot be relevant to the African. Its goal must be

> to interpret essential Christian faith in authentic African language in the flux and turmoil of our time so that there may be genuine dialogue between the Christian faith and African culture [Pobee 1979, 22].

Traditional religion is at the base of the African's religious feeling. It is through its practice that the African relates to the sublime. Thus,

> today, African Christians and missionaries alike are calling for an intensive study of the ingredients of the indigenous religious thought-forms and practices in order to ensure a truly effective communication of the Gospel [Fashole-Luke 1975, 259].

Theologians are aware that some of the traditional religious concepts touch the "soft spot" of the African quite readily. And the African looks to Christianity to supply some of the same help that traditional religion supplies. Appiah-Kubi tells us that "the most important single reason why people join the indigenous African Christian churches is HEALING" (1979, 117). This is why I contend that the genius of African theology lies in a translation that speaks to the African believers at the point of their religiosity.

There should, nevertheless, be theological continuity between the Christian faith and African traditional religion.[12] A Christian theology can develop from aspects of the African worldview that express traditional religious feelings,[13] provided that they are consistent with the gospel.

Some theologians would incorporate aspects of African culture. According to this school of thought:

> An African theologian should be a person who participates in African culture. . . . African culture becomes a crucial factor in doing theology with and for the African Christian community [Kurewa 1975, 37].

Many would share Mbiti's view that theology should be developed and expressed through African symbols, color, art, music, and sculpture.

Since we cannot do theology in a vacuum, we must employ the African cultural matrix (Mbiti 1978a, 33ff.).

In order to be Africanized, Christian theology must draw its nuances and concepts from the "systems of beliefs of the religion-based cultures of Africa" (Shorter 1977, 27). Yet, simply to rehash Christian tenets does not create African theology. What is needed are "those insights which are precious and original" (Shorter 1977, 27). One insight peculiarly African may be found in the concept of community (Sawyerr 1971a, 20). The community has a tremendous capacity to mold the individual. It builds one's personality, including spirituality and personal identity. "The attitude to birth and death, sin, sickness, forgiveness, and health all converge on the central role of the community" (Sawyerr 1971a, 20). It has been said that

> to talk of community is to imply the juxtaposition of persons in the *Imago Dei*. They are by that fact willynilly relating to one another. That requires the awareness of the existence of the other person and, therefore, of the community [Mbiti 1976a, 79].

In the teaching of love of neighbor, the concept of sharing, and the possibility of the ideal community of the believers, the African traditional community serves as a theological background in which love and respect, rather than rules and regulations, govern human conduct.

Sin against a fellow human being disrupts the smooth flow of community life. It upsets the communal status quo. In traditional Africa, "The important sins were those that damaged the relationships of the community" (Taylor 1963, 100). Against such a background African theology is reformulating new concepts of collective sin rather than focusing on individual sin.[14]

The spirit of community has a specific function, and its value for African theology cannot be overestimated. "The real value of a 'Theologia Africana' is more likely to be one of function than a strictly new content" (Sawyerr 1971b, 21). The function is defined by the African community from which theology draws its insights and to which it is accountable.

I believe that African theology is accountable to two authorities: (1) God, as revealed in various forms to different people, and (2) the community. It was out of a community that the biblical Word of God was written. The Bible is related to African theology as a record of how the Hebrew community experienced God and how the latter's self-revelation was manifested to the community.

The Bible

There is no Christian theologian in Africa who denies the fact that the Bible is a primary and basic source for any Christian theology (Fashole-Luke 1975, 263). Biblical teachings are being combined with, and compared with, African traditional religious concepts (Appiah-Kubi and Torres 1979, 88). John Mbiti's *New Testament Eschatology* (1972b) follows a method of juxtaposing the Bible with African traditional religion on the subject of eschatology.

The theologians who assembled at Immanuel College at Ibadan in 1966 set for themselves "the task of finding an answer to the delicate question of whether there is any correlation between the biblical concept of God and the African concept of God" (Dickson and Ellingworth 1971, 16). The anticipated outcome would be a Christian theology because the raw materials of tradition are reinterpreted in the light of the gospel, making the latter of relevance to the African people.

Given that the Bible is a primary source for African theology, theologians need to employ a special hermeneutic to produce a theology that speaks to the African people (McVeigh 1974b, 4). We are cautioned that "such Biblical theology will have to reflect the African situation and understanding" (Mbiti 1972b, 189). This word of caution indicates that not every scriptural passage necessarily speaks to every African situation all the time. For instance, although "Ethiopia shall soon stretch out her hands unto God" (Psalm 68:31) has been made the basis of some African indigenous churches (Sundkler 1961, 39), that call is not repeated forever.

The African Independent Churches

African theologians turn to the independent church movement for raw materials for their work because the independent churches do indigenize the Christian faith. In fact, most of them have been founded in order to meet the African's spiritual need through African traditional methods. Sawyerr is right when he writes:

> The independent churches have pointed the way to adaptations of Christian worship to suit the African worldview. But in their present

stage of development, no clear theological thinking has yet been
evolved by them [1971a, 24].

Leaders of African independent churches are not keen about writing
their respective theologies, but devote all their time to religious activities that include saving lives, curing the sick, and making the lame
walk. They do not believe in abstractions. The concept of self-reliance
is a case in point. While the Christian theologians in our mission
churches are working on theological support for the moratorium, the
indigenous African Christian church leaders are actually practicing
self-reliance. In fact, in some cases the independent church is a drama-
tization of the need for a moratorium on missionaries and foreign
funds. The Kimbanguist Church, for instance, has become one of the
largest self-supporting churches in Africa. It has its own hospitals and
schools, including a theological school at Nkamba where the prophet
Kimbangu is buried (*AACC Bulletin*, 10). A Kimbangu official
proudly said: "Our church is financially self-sufficient. All our activities are financially supported by our members, most of whom are
workers and farmers with modest income" (*AACC Bulletin*, 10).

The teachings of independent churches are, generally speaking,
based on the Scriptures. Indigenous churches all over the continent
"believe very strongly in the Bible. Their theology, therefore, is essentially biblical theology" (Omoyajowo 1972, 10).

African Christians need to develop a theology that is evangelistic and
practical. Consequently, it would be futile for them to spend too much
time on abstract truths and theological speculations, without attempting to develop a practical theology that the African believer can live by.
African theologians must reinterpret the gospel because the way in
which it was taught by most missionaries and some conservative
Westernized Africans no longer speaks effectively to the African
(Appiah-Kubi 1974, 5).

African theology needs to deal with pneumatology. The indigenous
churches, or "spirit churches," do provide theologians with an abun-
dant supply of raw materials that are pertinent to that doctrine. Of particular importance is the firm belief of most of the indigenous churches
"that the phenomena which characterized the pentacostal experience
are still possible in our day" (Omoyajowo 1972, 11). Mission churches
tend to regard this as "fundamentalism," with negative connotations
(Appiah-Kubi and Torres 1979, 119).

I think it is important that a doctrine of the Holy Spirit be fomulated, since the African religious mood is generally spiritually oriented. Ancestrology needs to be articulated in the light of the Christian doctrine of the Holy Spirit.

We may conclude that the presence of Christianity for over a hundred years has given the church in Africa as a whole a Christian heritage, one which is gradually being Africanized, in both mission and independent churches.

The Christian Tradition

Because African theology is Christian, there is a sense in which the entire Christian tradition is the background for the present theological enterprise. It has been argued, and rightly so, that church fathers like Saint Augustine, Tertullian, and Cyprian were the actual founders of African theology. Without becoming too involved in this debate, I will offer some general comments on the subject.

Many Christian theologians in Africa who stand in the church tradition recognize the difficulties created by the importation of Western theology and liturgy. Nevertheless, they still want to be sure that *Theologia Africana* remains in the "mainstream of the tradition of the church" (Sawyerr 1971b, 21). Many African theologians, believing that Christian tradition should be an integral part of African theology, do not wish to be "isolated from the catholicity of the church" (Mbiti 1972b, 189). They do not wish to deny the importance of the Christian tradition; at the same time they do want to bring fresh insights into African Christianity.

A dual problem arises here. If the existing body of Christian theology is important for African theology, why formulate new theological concepts for the church in Africa? But, if existing Christian concepts are really relevant to the African Christians, why, then, has Christianity remained more or less alien to the African church?

It is this dilemma that has caused some African theologians to reread, reinterpret, and reformulate the faith in language that is meaningful to the people.

For us Africans, as for others in the Christian tradition, theology must be contextual. Though it is true that there are aspects of Christian theology that may be above contextual definition, other aspects are necessarily related to their surroundings.

The church fathers undoubtedly made a tremendous contribution to Christian theology, of which African theology is a part. Since any efficacious theology cannot be neutral, the church fathers in question must have created theology to meet the need of their social context—precolonial and pre-neocolonial Africa. There are, therefore, some issues discussed then that have some relevance for us today, for instance, Augustine's "On the Free Will." Yet there are other issues that would not help shape a new future in post-neocolonial Africa. In light of this healthy balance, which incidentally justifies the debate, it can be said that while the church fathers could not have done African theology for our present context (which did not exist then), they do belong to a category of the founders of Christian theology. That fact cannot be debated.

Consequently, some of their work can provide a foundation for African theology providing that all the criteria for one who can do African theology in the present meaning of the term have been met. One of the criteria is that African theology be produced by theologians with a genuine African outlook. It cannot be produced just by the fact that the author is on the continent. African theology is not defined merely by geography. The purpose of African theology is to present the gospel in a more intelligible manner to Africans and to deal effectively with problems and situations peculiarly African.

I suggest that the faith that results, if it is based on the Scriptures, could bring new insights to other parts of Christendom.

DEFINITION

Several definitions of African theology have been put forward. Some have offered tentative definitions; others have defined African theology quite clearly and have not been apologetic about it.

John Kurewa's tentative definition of African theology is as follows:

African theology [is] the study that seeks to reflect upon and express the Christian faith in African thought-forms and idiom as it is experienced in African Christian communities, and always in dialogue with the rest of Christendom [1975, 36].

This definition emphasizes belonging to the mainstream as well as using African thought-forms, though it does not emphasize being biblical. There is a concern here, too, for African theology to emerge from the African cultural context.

John Mbiti defines African theology as "theological reflection and expression by African Christians" (1979a, 83). He says African theology thus defined "has to do with the presence and experience of the Christian faith among African people" (1978a, 33).

Appiah-Kubi prefers to label what everyone else calls *African theology* as "contextual African Biblical theology" (1974, 6). He joins hands with E. E. Mshana in maintaining that "African theology [is] a theology which emerges from the life, culture, traditions, and faith of the African peoples in their particular African context" (4). Appiah-Kubi further contends that African theology should be practical and relevant to the African people's needs. It should be situational, activist, dynamic, and liberating (6).

Aylward Shorter's definition of African Christian theology is rather elusive, but he correctly understands African theology as indigenized Christian theology (1977, 27). It is "a theology suited to modern national cultures which are essentially poly-ethnic in character, striving to weld together into unity a variety of traditions, . . . it is pluriform" (28).

After the 1966 Ibadan theological consultation, the AACC arranged for another consultation on which occasion a tentative definition of African Christian theology was agreed upon. It was stated at the Abidjan 1969 AACC assembly that

> By African theology we mean a theology which is based on the Biblical faith and speaks to the African "soul" (or is relevant to Africa). It is expressed in categories of thought which arise out of the philosophy of the African peoples [AACC 1970, 114].

In this definition "the emphasis is basically on *Christian* theology."[15] Also, according to this definition, African theology seeks "to create the 'new man' and community of Africa" (AACC 1970, 115). Mention of the African "soul" gives it a slightly new angle, but how to implement this definition is unclear.

All these definitions attempt to respond to a mandate to construct a biblically-based and relevant theology that speaks to the spiritual needs of the African people. The implication is obvious. Imported theologies did not touch the hearts of the African believers because they were couched in a religious language foreign to them. Hence the quest for a relevant African Christian theology. Furthermore, the cultural factor means that it is best that only African theologians undertake the task.

The foreign researcher, however sincere or experienced he may be, faces the danger of taking his own religion or point of view as normative. Hence the need for Africans to be interpreters and architects of "African Theology" [Appiah-Kubi 1974, 4].

I have quoted such a variety of definitions of African theology that it must be clear that a conclusive definition has not been established yet, since this theology is still in process. But because I have been able to trace its sources in some detail and give hints as to its content, it is now possible to define and spell out the content of African theology.

CONTENT

We can say with some confidence that African theology contains the experience of the African people as they know God and Christ. This experience ranges, naturally, from the personal and communal experiences stemming from traditional beliefs to acceptance of the central message of Jesus Christ and the experience of his liberating presence (Luke 4:18). Mbiti, among others, insists that Christian theology "has no interest in reading liberation into every text" (1974, 44), contending that "African theology . . . grows out of our joy in the experience of the faith" (43). But, we may ask, if liberation, or the salvation for which Christ came into the world, is not central to this theology, what is the reason for the rejoicing? It seems to me that the experience of liberation by Christ is the essential content of African theology.

It remains for the theologians to work out their doctrines gradually, relating Christianity to African tradition, and presenting them in terms that are acceptable and meaningful to the people.

A CRITICAL EVALUATION

It is not clear why African scholars and the AACC have found it necessary to develop an African theology when they are concerned that they *remain within the Christian traditional theological mainstream.* They say that African Christianity should not continue to receive prefabricated doctrines and liturgies of Western Christianity. Could it be that the scholars and AACC officials recognize some difficulties inherent in the Christianity that was presented by the missionaries? Yet African theologians are seeking African theological particularity within the broader Christian framework. It seems to me that the quest for an African theology cannot succeed as long as the major exponents continue to use the same theological methodologies that were used to construct mainstream theology. I suggest that African theologians need to develop new theological methods and tools.

I perceive four problems confronting the church today in Africa: (1) The Christian faith has remained largely alien to African believers in spite of the increasing number of Christians in Africa. A relevant African theology is needed in order to establish *continuity* between African traditional life and the new faith. (2) Having been colonized for several decades, many African people have lost their sense of *identity* and human dignity. The task of African theology is to help fulfill their African sense of humanity. This has not been accomplished. (3) The church in Africa constantly finds itself in changing sociopolitical situations. A theology of the church's responses and involvements is needed. The AACC has sponsored consultations, hoping that an African theology will provide a more meaningful *interpretation of the times*. (4) The African church needs to establish its own *theology of mission*. But first it has to be weaned from the missionary-sending churches of Europe and America. The problem is that the so-called parent churches find it difficult to let go. At the same time, an African theology is expected to articulate the moratorium issue and attempt to discover the present mission of the African church.

We will briefly discuss these four problems: continuity, identity, interpretation, and mission.

Continuity

African theologians are looking in the right direction when they attempt to formulate Christian theological tenets within the framework of traditional religion. The difficulty I see is that they are using Western theological tools in doing African theology. Consequently, they come up with a merely academic theology that is not relevant to African spirituality. However, this is only a part of the problem.

Unless the theologians first establish how they arrive at truth, any attempts to do a genuine African theology will be in vain. How African people interpret a piece of biblical literature depends on the African sociopolitical-religious context (Fueter 1956).

Theology, if there is to be continuity with traditional religion, must be responsive to African cosmology and a worldview centered on a concern for survival, for, unless any given "truth" leads to or enhances survival, it cannot be deemed crucial for the African. The average African is not concerned about abstractions; insights established in the light of God's grace and justice must have practical significance. Therefore, from my point of view, African theology is meaningful only if it enhances everyday life. If it cannot do that, then the gospel it preaches cannot be the word of *life*. A Christocentric African theology will articulate what Christ means for the African when he says: "I am the way, the truth, and the life" (John 14:6a). This brings us to the question of the African identity as it relates to Jesus Christ.

Identity

That Christianity was planted in Africa during the period of colonization was unfortunate. As we noted earlier, the people who evangelized among the Africans worked very closely with the colonizers. In most cases, they and the colonizers were of the same national and racial origin. The progress of African spiritual growth was not enhanced by the coming of Christianity under these circumstances; it was disrupted and distorted. Theology must, to establish and preserve the identity of the African people, resist any tendencies toward domination and dehumanization. But in order to make an effective protest, theologians must learn to make use of African tools.

Unless a characteristically African epistomology governs their articulation of "the way, the truth and the life," these theologians will not be able to present Jesus Christ in the most relevant manner. The Africans, themselves, can, and should, define what "the life" means for the people. But theology can help them discover who they really are in light of the teaching of Christ.

Interpretation of the Times

A third problem relates to the church's praxis. When the church is confronted with a theological problem, an African response, based on

African interpretation, is called for. Unless the African church develops a distinctly African theology, how can the problem in question be solved? Some of the difficulties the church faces may actually have been caused by the application of Christian principles. It is not realistic to expect Western culture to solve problems for which it is responsible. For example, the African church is having difficulties with the cash economy. Is there no alternative to running the church with grants?

The African church needs a framework within which people may understand and actively respond to political, social, and religious issues. While the AACC can act as the mouthpiece of the church, it needs theological handles if it is to maintain a consistent African worldview. The African church should decompartmentalize African life in order to recapture the holistic philosophy which is a genuine African lifestyle.

Mission

The fourth problem is related to the other three. The African church has been expanding physically, but, as I have noted, its spiritual growth has been stifled by the persistent presence of the missionaries, together with foreign aid from the parent churches. The African church has been too long an object of mission for Christians of other nations.

The African church itself needs to develop a theology of mission. The church cannot remain dependent on the parent church indefinitely. The church needs to reformulate its self-understanding so that it may genuinely know itself as a part of Christ's mission in the world. What is our direct response to Christ's command to follow and love him? We have the poor, the oppressed, and the sick among us; what is our Christian response to the least of these, our brothers and sisters? An articulation of our response to these questions indicates our theology of mission.

My conclusion is that African theologians, while correctly observing the need for Africanization and indigenization, have yet to come up with an appropriate methodology and a relevant theological perspective.

Chapter 8

Black Theology in South Africa

Black theology[1] is an important African voice within the Third World. It is a Christian theology, since its exponents are Christians who are reflecting upon a situation of extreme oppression by white racist people. In dealing with their situation, the makers of black theology in South Africa (whom I shall call black theologians) are concerned about three matters: African humanity, Christian faith, and political liberation. Black theologians are advocating a black theology that focuses on the survival of African people.

Many articles have been written on black theology in South Africa. These will serve as the sources for our interpretation. There are only a few books on black theology in South Africa. Important works are *The Challenge of Black Theology in South Africa* (1974), edited by Basil Moore,[2] and *Farewell to Innocence: A Socio-ethical Study on Black Theology and Power* (1977), written by Allan Boesak.[3] *The Church Struggle in South Africa* (de Gruchy 1979) is significant because it gives a history of the South African church, the context within which black theology is being done.

Among the authors of articles on black theology in South Africa, I will focus on the major voices of Bishop Desmond Tutu, Manas Buthelezi, and Allan Boesak. Other authorities will be cited also, but these three will be our chief resources because they are undoubtedly the prominent voices at the present time.

Desmond Tutu has written several articles, including "Black Theology" (1974b), "The Theology of Liberation in Africa" (1979), and "Black Theology/African Theology: Soul Mates or Antagonists?'' (1975). The most influential essays of Manas Buthelezi are "An African Theology or Black Theology?'' (1974a) and "Toward Indigenous Theology in South Africa'' (1978).

A more recent but increasingly significant voice is Allan Boesak. In addition to *Farewell to Innocence* (1977) he has written "Liberation Theology in South Africa'' (1979). These select articles and books by black South Africans have been especially significant in the defining and shaping of black theology in South Africa. Since our purpose here is to describe the development of black theology in the South African context, we will first discuss its sources.

SOURCES

The term *black theology* in South Africa was borrowed from North American black theologians.[4] John de Gruchy is right in his observation that "the earliest articulation of black theology under that title was primarily the work of the American theologian James Cone'' (1979, 153), whose first book on the subject appeared in 1969.

However, by the time this terminology was generally adopted, the content of black theology was already in existence in South Africa. This means that the sources of black theology in South Africa are different from those in North America, although there may be similarities. In fact, this connection is natural, and since the nineteenth century there has been exchange of religious and political ideas between the black Christians in South Africa and their black brothers and sisters in North America.[5]

My immediate interest here is to identify the sources of black theology. From where does black theology draw its theological insights? I perceive three major sources: the Bible, the South African black experience, and the North American black theological heritage.

The Bible

Black theology is a biblical theology expressing itself contextually. James Cone says that "Black theology is kerygmatic theology. That is, it is theology that takes seriously the importance of Scripture in theological discourse'' (1970, 66). Allan Boesak agrees with Cone that black theology is a theology of liberation which believes that "liberation is not only 'part of' the gospel, or 'consistent with' the gospel, it is the gospel of Jesus Christ" (Boesak 1978, 76).

Bishop Desmond Tutu, responding to charges that black theology is unbiblical, argues that many black theologians have "had a real encounter with Jesus Christ in prayer, meditation, Bible study, and the Sacraments." Tutu adds that "the imperatives of this encounter constrain us to speak and to act as we do. It is not our politics but our faith that inspires us" (1979, 168).

Allan Boesak demonstrates that black theology draws its raw material as well as its theme of liberation from the Bible. According to him, "the theme of liberation is already present in Genesis 15:14 and it is evident right through the Old Testament in the preaching of the prophets as a fundamental fact of redemption" (1977, 17–18). Tutu's article makes the important observation that as theology in the Bible is an "engaged" theology, so black theology is also "engaged," "an involved theology" (1979, 164). In fact, Tutu points out that "the ultimate reference point is the man Jesus who is the Word of God par excellence" (1979, 165).

Black liberation theology has challenged other theologies "to examine whether they are biblical in the sense in which liberation theology has been shown to be biblical" (Tutu 1979, 168). Although not many scriptural passages are quoted by some of the black liberation theologians, the impact of this theology is "more truly incarnational by being concerned for the whole person, body and soul" (Tutu 1979, 168). Boesak informs us that

each theological concept develops within a particular context, and . . . our theological thinking—the way we read the Gospel, the way we understand the Gospel, the way we interpret the Gospel, the way we interpret our situation in light of the Gospel— . . . profoundly influences the way we do our theology [Tutu 1979, 171–72].

Thus black theology is localized in the South African religious context.

Even though it is situational, "for black theology, it is the Christian faith that determines how to relate to the sociopolitical situation, not the situation which determines the faith" (de Gruchy 1979, 166). The word of God is the norm, not social praxis or culture. Boesak reminds us that the themes of liberation theology that have become so important to black and native American Christians in the U.S., to people in Asia and Latin America, are the same themes that run through black liberation theology in South Africa [1979, 173].

The Bible inspires the oppressed peoples to continue to struggle. Consequently it is believed that the God who liberated Israel from Egypt will also liberate people from the oppression of today. Because of this conviction, black theologians are committed to their faith and their God, who alone can deliver them from bondage.

Black Experience

The experience of the blacks is also one of the major sources of black theology in South Africa. In fact, the black experience in South Africa and that in North America come very close to being the same; hence the dialogue between the two continents (Wilmore and Cone 1979, 446). James Cone speaks for many when he says that "our cultural continuity with black people in Africa, the Caribbean, and Latin America should enable us to talk with each other about common hopes and dreams in politics and economics" (446).

There are, however, sufficient sociocultural differences to warrant independent developments of black theology in the two regions. For instance the form of slavery has been different. While in South Africa blacks experience psychological slavery and economic exploitation, in North America they have been actually legally enslaved. The point here is not to compare cultures or political structures, but to demonstrate that the social contexts in the two regions are not identical.

Black theology in South Africa comes out of a suffering black community. Most African black theologians observe that color is a crucial factor.

In South Africa the black man knows and feels the crunch of his suffering at the point of his blackness. He is completely justified, therefore, in claiming that he is suffering because of his blackness [Moore 1974, 23].

Suffering because one is black can only be felt and experienced by members of the black community. Consequently, black experience is a peculiar phenomenon which has necessitated a black liberation theology.

It is this black experience out of which black theology is emerging. Therefore, what black South Africans experience influences how they hear and read the Word of God. Black African theologians contend that experience "determines the hermeneutical setting for the Word of God" (Moore 1974, 33), which is designed to liberate the suffering in their social context.

Other black South African theologians correctly maintain that their theology comes out of the experience of "obedience to the Gospel amid the realities of contemporary suffering, racism, oppression, and everything else that denies the lordship of Christ" (de Gruchy 1979, 160). This contradiction between obedience to the liberator and continued suffering has resulted in reflective thinking which is nourished by the promise of Christ's ultimate triumph. In a Christ-centered theology of liberation, the belief is that, in the end, Christ and his own will triumph over any sort of evil and suffering. Victory is certain.

Black theology, according to Buthelezi, does not come out of libraries or reminiscences of "the good old days."[6] It comes from reflections upon the painful experiences of "the one whom we see in Johannesburg, Durban, and Cape Town trying to make ends meet in the framework of Influx-Control legislation" (Buthelezi 1978, 64). Thus, black theology is coming out of the live experience of miserable and extremely oppressive social surroundings.

Black Theological Heritage

Black theology in South Africa was planted, taught, and debated in the universities, student associations, and churches. Much of it had come from James Cone's "original expositions of the subject" which became "known to black theological students in South Africa" (de Gruchy 1979, 153). The church became involved in black consciousness as a movement. As a result, black theology "gained considerable prominence through the University Christian Movement (UCM) in the late sixties" (de Gruchy 1979, 153). The UCM had been formed in 1966,[7] the year generally held to be the date of birth of black theology in North America.

Black theology was first institutionalized by the UCM, which sponsored "a series of seminars on black theology" in South African institutions of learning (de Gruchy 1979, 155). From these consultations and seminars there emerged the first South African book on black theology.[8] Ironically, the banning of this book, its sponsors, and project directors by the white South African government gave black theology even more publicity.

There is unanimous agreement among black theologians that

> in South Africa, black theology was inspired by its North American counterpart, which existed for so long implicitly in the Negro spirituals that gave heart to black slaves in the heavy days of their bondage and which became more articulate and explicit during the civil rights campaign [Tutu 1979, 163–64].

The African independence "fever" also helped to install black theology in South Africa (Tutu 1979, 164). By 1973 black theology had been planted in South Africa.

DEFINITION

Basil Moore offers this definition of black theology in South Africa: "Black theology is a situational theology. And the situation is that of the Black man in South Africa" (1973, 5). Moore has also defined it as a theology searching for new symbols with which to affirm black humanity. "It is a theology of the oppressed, by the oppressed, for the liberation of the oppressed" (ix).

To comprehend the meaning of black theology in South Africa, these definitions must be understood as two different ways of stating the same truth. As a theology of liberation, not only does it direct its voice to the oppressed black people, but it hopes that the white oppressors will also hear the good news and be saved (Moore 1973, 139).

Thus, liberation means a new life, a liberated existence for both the hitherto oppressed and their former oppressors. According to this new life, to "love your neighbor as yourself" means, for the black South Africans, "love your brother and affirm him, but do not make him more than you" (Moore 1973, 139). Black theologians understand that the gospel of Jesus Christ not only calls black South Africans to freedom but also "calls to limitless forgiveness, not as a spineless acceptance of suffering but as participation in the divine economy of salvation" (Appiah-Kubi and Torres 1979, 167). Liberation does not seek to tip the balance, but to strike a state of social equilibrium.

Black theology is also defined as "an attempt by black Christians to grasp and think through the central claims of the Christian faith in the light of the black experience (Mgojo 1973, 28). Most of the black theologians believe that the Word of God, rather than just blackness, is the criterion of black theology in South Africa. John de Gruchy, a white theologian, observes that this choice of a criterion makes a great distinction between black theology in North America and that in South Africa.[9] In South Africa, most black theologians contend that as a situational theology, black theology

> is the black people's attempt to come to terms theologically with their black situation. It seeks to interpret the gospel in such a way that the situation of blacks will begin to make sense [Boesak 1977, 13].

There is another perspective that defines black theology. Speaking for himself as well as other black South Africans, Desmond Tutu declares:

> I myself believe I am an exponent of Black theology, coming as I do from South Africa. I also believe I am an exponent of African theology, coming as I do from Africa. I contend that Black theology is like the inner and smaller circle in a series of concentric circles. . . . I and others from South Africa do Black theology, which is for us, at this point, African theology [Wilmore and Cone 1979, 490].

According to this view, African theology, like liberation theology, is regarded as an umbrella under which are found various theologies, including black theology.

This definition has interesting dynamics. By arguing that black theology is a smaller circle within the greater circle (African theology), black theologians retain their African identity. Also, since African theologians claim to be Christian and biblical in their theology, it follows that black theology must also be accepted as being both biblical and Christian. I make this point because there are a few African theologians who prefer to dissociate themselves from black theology, which, they allege, is unbiblical and, by implication, unchristian.[10]

The fact of theological coexistence between black and African theologies has healthy implications for a dialogue between North American black theology and African theology.[11] Although some African theologians speak of black theology as unbiblical and too preoccupied with politics,[12] most black South Africans believe that black theology is African theology. More precisely, black theology is an aspect of African theology. However, black theology is not identical with African theology, because the former's characteristics do not all coincide with those of the latter.

MAJOR CHARACTERISTICS

Three major characteristics of black theology are illustrated by the definitions offered above: (1) An emphasis on *liberation* distinguishes black theology from other African theologies of which it is a part. (2) It is a *biblically based* theology. In fact, emphasis on liberation enhanced by Jesus Christ the Liberator, makes the Scriptures a very important ingredient of black theology. And (3) it is *contextual*. The social context of black theology is that of the black South African situation.

Liberation

All black theologians in South Africa share the view that they are oppressed because they are black. However, they also believe that God, who created them black, is the liberator of those who are oppressed because of the color of their skin. This makes Christ the Liberator central to black theology. Because he represents both vicarious suffering and liberation, Jesus Christ brings a message that is desperately needed in South Africa. Black theology, therefore, is the interpretation of what Christ has to say about the oppressed and their liberation. And liberation is an aspect of the salvation brought by Christ.

The gospel is good news for the black South Africans because its message brings a new light to dehumanized and oppressed people. For them, love becomes a major ingredient in their struggle for liberation. As Christ liberates because he loves all humanity, so the oppressed must love even their oppressors, not to mention each other. Black theologians believe that "God's love is an active deed of liberation manifested in divine power" (Boesak 1977, 95). Love, not hate, revenge, or hostility, characterizes South African black theology. In fact, love distinguishes black theology of liberation from liberation in other contexts. Here the power of Jesus Christ, who liberates, also sustains the suffering black people until their full humanity is accomplished through liberation.

To identify liberation as an important characteristic of black theology is also to affirm that the latter is a Christian movement intending to stress the liberation of those who are oppressed. With the love of God, liberation has taken effect. In fact, love precedes liberation. Christ sets the suffering free because he loves them and has the power to set at liberty those who are in prison, the poor, and the oppressed (Luke 4:18–21). This is why black theology takes liberation very seriously. Christianity makes sense to the oppressed people in South Africa because of the faith's central message of liberation.

Biblical Basis

Black theology is biblically based, teaching that, through Christ, God has been revealed as caring about humanity. The Scriptures tell the story of God's love and power to liberate the oppressed. This has led the oppressed to believe that, because God liberated Israel, God will liberate them also. Because God's name is "I am who I am," black theology believes that God will always participate in history.

The three major theologies in Africa seem to have three different theological emphases, based on prevailing need and interpretation. Like other Third World theologies, black theology seeks to be relevant to the need for liberation of the oppressed black masses, whose very existence is at stake. While liberation is crucial for the oppressed blacks, survival is decisive for African traditional theology. For African theology, salvation is the crucial concern. Theologians in the mainstream of Christianity regard Christ as Lord, not because he is the Liberator, but because he saves us from sin. There is, however, a relation between liberation and salvation. Both stem from the power of Jesus Christ. Christ the Liberator died on the cross so that sinful humanity might be saved from inhuman conditions, such as oppression, dehumanization, exploitation, poverty, and hate.

Black South Africans need to be saved from oppression that has been imposed on them by the white South Africans. However, such salvation cannot remain abstract. It needs to take concrete dimensions in the form of political liberation so that blacks can experience what it is to be fully human.

Black theology places much emphasis on this biblically based theme of liberation, because it alleviates the burden of oppression. The biblical teachings about God and his salvific work in history draw black South African theologians closer to God who has the kind of power that they need to carry their burden and assure survival. The Bible has many themes; it is up to theologians to pursue what speaks to their social context.

Contextualization

Black theology is contextual. This means that it seeks to speak to the oppressed black people in their situation. Contextual theology "does not mean mere conformity to the past and present situations, but critical and prophetic confrontation with the movement of history" (Kaufmann 1973, 251). A contextual theology seeks to reread the Bible and apply a contextualized interpretation of the Scripture's message. Black theology is effective in concretizing and particularizing the good news to the oppressed, the poor, and the suffering.

Black South African theologians agree that their theology is situational because they realize that the situation in South Africa is unique. Although it has been suggested that African theology be labeled "contextual African Biblical Theology" (Appiah-Kubi 1974, 6), not many theologians seem to accept such a label. By implication, they place less emphasis on contextualization than do black theologians.[13]

A CRITICAL EVALUATION

Black theology has been subjected to heavy criticism by many theologians in Africa. In evaluating it here, I will attempt to ascertain whether the criticism is valid or not. I employ two criteria in evaluating black theology. First: Is it a faithful presentation of the gospel of Jesus Christ? Second: Does it speak for the black oppressed people of South Africa, where this theology is prevalent? To answer these two questions, we have to examine the major sources of black theology.

As suggested earlier, there are three major sources of black theology, one of which is the Bible. Because of this biblical basis, some black theologians have legitimately argued that "Christian theology is a theology of liberation" (Cone 1970, 17). Boesak supports this position. He says, "The message of liberation forms the *cantus firm-*

us of the proclamation of the New Testament" (Boesak 1977, 20).

If, then, liberation is a central Christian message, how do black theologians understand it in view of the oppressive situation they find themselves in? All evidence points to the fact that since Christ is the center of the Christian message, what he stood for, namely the liberation of the oppressed (Luke 4:18–21), becomes the central message of black theology. This theme of liberation is not just a New Testament phenomenon. "This liberation message was the center and sustenance of the life of Israel" (Boesak 1977, 18). Thus, the theme of liberation comes to us from both the Old Testament and the New Testament (Exod. 19:4, 5; Ps. 72; Deut. 7:7; Lk. 4:18–21).

In light of all this biblical evidence and bases, it is not fair to say, as some African theologians do, that there is too much emphasis on "liberation" in black theology. On the contrary, one is inclined to reverse such thinking and locate liberation as the major contribution of black theology. Therefore the good news black theology proclaims to the oppressed is the message that God has taken sides with them (Cone 1970, 22). God has heard their crying. This leads us to the next question.

Does black theology speak for the black oppressed communities in the world? Yes. James Cone clearly states that

insofar as Black Theology is a theology arising from an identification with the oppressed black community and seeks to interpret the gospel of Jesus Christ in the light of the liberation of that community, it is Christian theology [1970, 25].

In addition to what Cone says, I agree with Moore that black theology speaks for the oppressed black communities because it is a theology of the black people, by the black people, and for the black people (Moore 1973, ix). Consequently black theology is best done only by blacks themselves. It is not just an academic exercise.

Because black experience is one of the major sources of black theology, color is an important prerequisite for the doing of black theology. Black theology can be regarded as "authentic Christian theology" (Cone 1970, 25) because it is arising from the black churches themselves. Because their suffering is indigenous to them, so are their theological thinking and reflections.

Black theology is not a prefabricated theology. It is created by the black Christians in the light of the Scriptures as they are read and interpreted by blacks themselves. Even in the case of South Africa, where the term *black theology* is known to have been imported from North America, the actual theological content is constructed contextually in order to speak more specifically to the black South African situation.

Thus black theology is being done in particular social contexts to deal with respective dehumanizing and oppressive forces, principalities and powers. The fact that black theology is being done contextually should not imply that it lacks universal dimensions. On the one hand, its universality is based on the fact that Christ, its center, is universal. On the other hand, its particularity is based on the fact that "blackness" is a concrete reality, which is the point at which the black people are oppressed.

Black theology has also dealt with the question of black identity, which is directly related to the issue of color. In fact, black theology has been opposed because of its emphasis on color. Is God color-conscious? Cone says that

> God is never color blind. To say God is color blind is analogous to saying that God is blind to justice and injustice, to right and wrong, to good and evil. Certainly this is not the picture of God revealed in the Old and New Testaments [1970, 25].

Black theologians have fought the white people's racist attitude toward blackness. All the imagery and symbols of blackness were meant to convey evil. Black theology has attempted to give an authentic and positive interpretation of what God has created in God's own image.

Black theologians cannot depend on other people's interpretation of the Scriptures any more. Who can better interpret what it means to be black than the black people themselves? As noted earlier, experience is a very authentic source of black theology because God's children meet God in their daily experience.

The overall experience of the black people has a religious and spiritual background in the African traditional religion. Although some South African black theologians (Torres and Fabella 1978, 65–6) tend to reject African traditional religion, I contend that the latter has some influence on black experience because black theology is the inner circle of African theology, the outer circle.

On the one hand, it is true that blacks should be skeptical when white missionaries urge them to go back to the "good old days," because it is important for blacks to deal with the present realities. However, today's realities are tomorrow's past. I believe that no people can afford to divorce themselves from their past nor should they divorce themselves from the present and live purely in the past. There should be a degree of continuity in the faith from the past to the present and the future.

On the other hand, since the black people of South Africa are as much African as any other Africans (especially south of the Sahara), there is no reason why black theologians cannot utilize traditional African beliefs to enhance their Christian worship and theological concepts. Already African theology is drawing heavily from the traditional religion. It is not clear to me why the latter should be rejected in developing a black theology with roots in the African experience.

I agree with black theologians who contend that "black theology must come out of the black church. And the black church comes out of black religion. And black religion comes out of the African experience."[14]

While it is true that black theology must confront white domination with means equal to those of the oppressors, it is also true that the only way black South Africans can attain their full humanity and dignity is to incorporate the African cultural heritage.

In fact, political liberation alone does not make a people. Black theology needs to interpret liberation in such a way that it applies to anything that fails the development of a full African humanity. Black theology should call for political liberation as well as cultural liberation, that is, freedom to adopt those aspects of African traditional life which help build up the dehumanized blacks in diaspora.

When black theology has dealt adequately with the three concerns mentioned at the beginning of this chapter, it will have accomplished a major goal. That is, however, by no means the end result of black theology. Black liberation theology is an ongoing process. Black theology has already made a tremendous contribution to Christendom in general and to the Third World in particular.

Notes

Chapter 1: African Traditional Religion

1. I shall draw mostly from these three authors but I will also occasionally cite other Africans and non-Africans who have made some contribution to either African traditional religion or African theology or both. Non-Africans such as Geoffrey Parrinder, Aylward Shorter, and Malcolm J. McVeigh have made important studies in this field. See their special contributions in the Bibliography.

2. Besides the works mentioned in this chapter, Mbiti has published numerous articles on African traditional religions and African theology.

3. These African peoples use the pronoun *It,* rather than a personal one, because for them God is neither male nor female. God is spirit.

4. There has been much debate about the role of natural theology in analyzing the meaning of the Christian view of God. Karl Barth is one of the few major theologians who rejected natural theology entirely. His radical rejection of natural theology was useful in his struggle against Nazism during the 1930s but not so useful in relating his theology to African traditional religion and Asian religions. I believe that it is impossible to hold a Barthian view of revelation that limits divine revelation to Jesus Christ and also use African traditional religion as a major source of African theology.

5. See John 1:1.

6. For further reading see Sawyerr 1966.

7. By syncretism, some African theologians mean a tendency to combine Christian and African traditional beliefs which, in their view, do not belong together. Others, however, see syncretism positively—as a means of reconciling Christian beliefs with traditional African beliefs. According to this school of thought, syncretism means that African traditional religion is enlightened by the special revelation.

8. See Genesis 1:31.

9. Even in those very rare cases where there is only one child in the family, one says *Baba vedu,* because there are cousins who also claim him as their father.

Chapter 2: The Coming of Christianity to Africa: The Nineteenth and Twentieth Centuries

1. E. B. Idowu writes from his own experience in his book *Towards an Indigenous Church* (1965). Mbiti does the same thing when he writes about "Africanizing" Christianity. See especially "The Encounter of Christian Faith and African Religion" (1980). K. Appiah-Kubi writes in a similar fashion about stripping Christianity of its Western theological garb or liberating the faith from Western clothes. See his "Why African Theology?" (1974).

2. The Conference of the Third World theologians released a final communiqué stating that the Bible is the basic ingredient of African theology (see Appiah-Kubi and Torres 1979, 81–142).

3. This is when Christianity reached as far as the Congo, where Alphonso's son Henry became the first ordained African bishop from sub-Saharan Africa (Lugira n.d., 53).

4. One of our white district superintendents actually served in the Rhodesian army as a police reservist at the same time that he was serving as a United Methodist missionary.

5. William Wadé Harris hailed from Cape Palmas in Liberia. He started a mass movement on the French Ivory Coast. "The Church of the Twelve Apostles" and the present Methodist Church on the Ivory Coast trace their origins to this Grebo (Kru) prophet William Wadé Harris. A fuller discussion about him properly comes in the chapter on the independent church movements. I only wish to note here that Harris came out of what seemed to be futile American missionary efforts in Liberia.

6. It is in Uganda that the All Africa Conference of Churches was inaugurated in 1963 as if the blood of the martyrs there was the seed of Christianity in Africa.

7. Most of the Old Testament ideals resemble those of traditional Africa. For instance, having children is the ideal in the Old Testament. Polygamy is often a solution to childlessness.

8. My father was among the first converts in the Rusape area. He remembers quite vividly how Africans worshipped God through their ancestors and also how Christianity was planted in the areas in Zimbabwe. His personal experiences have greatly enlightened me during this study.

Chapter 3: The African Independent Church Movement

1. Some theologians prefer to call these churches *indigenous* rather than *independent,* a term with a derogatory connotation (see Appiah-Kubi

1979, 117ff.). J. Omoyajowo also prefers to use the term *indigenous* rather than *independent*. Like Appiah-Kubi, Omoyajowo argues that the term *independent* suggests that there is some more important reference point outside these churches. (See especially Omoyajowo 1972.) Others who use the term *independent* simply inherit the traditional usage from the mission churches, which do regard these indigenous churches as having broken away from the major church. I prefer the term *independent* because it suggests that such churches are not dependent on missionary agents overseas. They are independent both ecclesiastically and economically; hence decision-making power rests within the churches, not outside them. This is the sense in which I use the term *independent* in this chapter. However, insofar as theology is seeking to be truly African, I also use the term *indigenous* to refer to the independent churches because they are of African origin and under African leadership. More important, these churches consciously tend to adopt certain agreeable traditional practices into their Christian worship.

2. A good example is Baeta's *Prophetism in Ghana* (1962).

3. Sundkler's *Bantu Prophets in South Africa* (1961) provides examples.

4. Ethiopian churches are, generally speaking, nationalistically inspired churches. There is more overt political awareness than in other forms of independency.

5. Zionism refers to independent churches that claim to have emanated from Mount Zion in Jerusalem. Theologically, they can be characterized as the faith-healing churches, which speak with tongues, engage in purification rites, and taboos. See Sundkler 1961, 53–64.

6. According to Hastings (1979), in Zimbabwe, Malawi, and Zambia, they are generally referred to as the prophetic or faith-healing churches.

7. Mabel Ensor was a white woman who started an independent church in October 1928. The movement collapsed because, according to Oosthuizen, "the Africans opposed this unconscious manifestation of Western superiority" (1968, 47).

8. Kimbanguism was founded in the 1920s but was only recognized in 1959, according to Parrinder. It now has a membership of over 3 million. The story is told that one night in 1918 when many Congolese Africans were dying of influenza, "Kimbangu heard a voice saying: 'I am Christ, my servants are unfaithful, I have chosen you to witness and convert your brothers. . . . Take care of my sheep' " (Hollenwager 1974, 59).

9. These two men had been laborers in the gold and diamond mines in South Africa. According to Hastings, they picked up Zionism and brought it home to Zimbabwe.

10. The call came to the founder while on his way from the city of Um-

tali to his home. Hastings writes: "Near Mt. Nyengwe he was suddenly conscious of a powerful light and a voice saying to him: 'You are John the Baptist, an Apostle. Now go and do my work! Tell them not to commit adultery, not to steal and not to become angry! Baptize people and keep the Sabbath Day' " (Daneel 1974, 319).

Chapter 4: African Nationalism

1. See, R. W. July 1970. DuBois deliberately chose Paris and the date to coincide with the Versailles Peace Conference so that the first congress would be held in the place where major European powers had assembled. July says DuBois wanted "to demonstrate the solidarity of the black race" (458).

2. According to R. W. July (1970), the American President Wilson had promised all who fought in the First World War that after the war, the principle of self-determination would be enforced. DuBois and other black people took that seriously and hoped that a new order would ensue, substituting freedom for paternalism. "It was this mood which characterized the Pan-African Congresses organized by the American Negro leader W. E. B. DuBois, which lent urgency to the program of J. E. Casely Hayford's National Congress of British West Africa, and which prompted nationalist leaders in their demands for extension of political rights, . . . equality of economic opportunity between the white man and the black" (R. W. July 1970).

3. Black American by birth, W. E. B. DuBois participated in the founding of the National Association for the Advancement of Colored People (NAACP). He organized the first Pan-African Congress in 1919. DuBois eventually became a citizen of independent Ghana, the first African state south of the Sahara to gain independence from the British. For a detailed account see S. A. Akintoye (1976) and R. W. July (1970).

4. According to R. W. July (1970), the first congress was held in Paris in 1919, the second in London, Brussels, and Paris in 1921. The third convened in London and Lisbon in 1923, when the Garvey movement emerged. In 1927 the congress met in New York City. However, according to Immanuel Geiss, the very first Pan-African meeting was held in 1900 in London. This means that the 1919 congress should then be counted as the second. This difference can be explained this way: Before 1919, Pan-African meetings were considered as merely an association, but as of 1919 they became known as congresses. See Geiss 1974, 192–240. Some historians consider the first All Africa Peoples' Conference, which met in Accra in December 1958, to be the sixth congress.

5. Jamaican by birth, Marcus Garvey founded the United Negro Im-

provement Association, with a platform emphasizing black separatism and return to Africa in the 1920s. For further readings on Garvey see Cronon (1969) and Jacques-Garvey ([1923–26] 1967). It is important to note that it was Garvey who was the chief advocate for the back-to-Africa movement.

6. In an article entitled "The Future—and . . . African Theology" by Professors J. H. Cone and Gayraud Wilmore, the authors made the claim that "Whatever our poets, writers, and statesmen have said about sources of African nationalism and Pan-Africanism, it was from religious men in Africa and the United States—from Paul Cuffee, Daniel Coker, Bishop Turner, Mangena Mokone, James M. Dwane, John Chilembure, Edward Blyden, and a host of others . . . that the religious vision of Africa's great destiny first arose and the initial call went out for the elevation and solidarity, under God, of all peoples of African descent." This article first appeared in *Pro Veritate* (Jan. 15–Feb. 15, 1972). It was later published in Massie 1973 and is also reprinted in Wilmore and Cone 1979.

7. Wilmot Blyden was West Indian in origin. Born in 1832, he settled in Liberia in 1851 and became editor of the Liberia *Herald*. He was ordained in the Presbyterian Church of West Africa and became a professor at Liberia College. Geiss notes that "all the way from Casely Hayford to Garvey, Padmore, and Nkrumah, Pan-African spokesmen time and again referred to Blyden . . ." (Geiss 1974, 150ff.).

8. Note that the All Africa Church Conference, which met in Ibadan, Nigeria, in 1958, made the same stipulation in the light of the spirit of nationalism within the church. This dream culminated when the AACC was inaugurated in Kampala in 1963. *The Drumbeats from Kampala* (1963), *Engagement: Abidjan 1969* (1970), and *The Struggle Continues* (1975) all report the African church's concern to be politically aware and involved in African affairs.

9. George Padmore was formerly known as Malcolm Ivan Meredith Nurse, born in Trinidad in 1903. Padmore always identified himself as "a nephew of the late Sylvester Williams, a West Indian barrister." He also had key posts in the International Trade Union Committee of Negro Workers, a Communist-related organization. For more information see Hooker 1967.

10. Akintoye's *Emergent African States* (1976) describes the rise of the modern African states to political independence. Richard Hull's *Modern Africa: Change and Continuity* (1980) gives the subject a more philosophical treatment. Basil Davidson's *Let Freedom Come: Africa in Modern History* (1978) is also useful. J. S. Coleman's *Nigeria: A Background to Nationalism* (1958) and T. Hodgkin's *Nationalism in Colonial Africa* (1956) give good background for what set the stage for political inde-

pendence in Africa following the series of congresses mentioned earlier. Basil Davidson's *Africa in History: Themes and Outlines* (1968) is also a good source.

11. I shall discuss moratorium in greater detail in chapter 5, where I talk about the All Africa Conference of Churches and the origin of African theology.

12. Burgess Carr's Lusaka address expresses the concern of both African theologians and nationalists that Africa has been too dependent for too long. "This dependence not only affects our self-image but poses a grave threat to the future of Christianity on our continent" (AACC 1975, 76).

13. General Walls, former Rhodesian White Army general, was reappointed to the same position by Prime Minister R. G. Mugabe (*The Herald*, May 1980).

14. See Nkrumah 1961; 1962. And on unity, Nkrumah 1967.

15. Rev. Ndabaningi Sithole is a nationalist leader of one of the factions in Zimbabwe, the Zimbabwe African National Union (ZANU). He is also an ordained minister of the Church of Christ. Bishop Abel Tendekayi Muzorewa, author of *Rise Up and Walk* (1978), is also the president of a faction in Zimbabwe. He was the nation's prime minister before it was recognized internationally. Bishop A. T. Muzorewa has been serving as both the bishop of the United Methodist Church of Zimbabwe (since 1968) and as the president of the United African National Council (since 1972).

16. See also Cone's *Black Theology and Black Power* (1969).

Chapter 5: The All Africa Conference of Churches

1. The All Africa Conference of Churches (AACC) is an ecumenical body that consists of at least one hundred different churches in Africa. It was founded on April 20, 1963, at Kampala, Uganda.

2. At its official inauguration, the AACC made concrete arrangements to sponsor the first theological consultation, which resulted in a book, *Biblical Revelation and African Beliefs* (Dickson and Ellingworth 1971).

3. The committee consisted of eleven members. Sir Francis Ibiam from Nigeria was the chairperson. Dr. Donald M'Timkulu was appointed the general secretary.

4. This body had determined from the beginning that the organization would be a black people's organization. L. B. Greaves reports that "great care was taken to ensure that the programs of the conference did not bear the trademark, 'made in Geneva.' It was worked out in Africa by a largely African committee in as much consultation as possible with the churches in each African territory" (1958, 257–263).

5. Between 1957 (when Ghana became independent) and 1963, more

than twenty-two formerly colonized African states won their independence. See Akintoye 1976 for a detailed account.

6. Regarding this book, John Mbiti comments: "The contents of the book have very little biblical material except for one essay on eschatology" (1979a, 85).

7. The reader will notice that I place more emphasis on Kampala and Abidjan than I do on the later conference at Lusaka. This is because our primary concern is the origin of African theology. Lusaka comes out of Kampala and Abidjan.

8. Besides these two, all other sources are sometimes quite controversial. For instance, Mbiti and his colleagues strongly recommend the Western Christian tradition of the church as a source of African theology. Others like Kofi Appiah-Kubi and some black theologians in South Africa will have nothing to do with the white Western tradition. In fact, they reject it as the worst enemy of African theology. See Mbiti's article in *All Africa Lutheran Consultation on Theology in the African Context* (Lutheran World Federation Department of Church Cooperation Oct. 5–14, 1978). See also Appiah-Kubi 1974.

9. Selfhood in this context is defined as "personality with separate conscious existence"; selfhood also means identity (AACC 1963, 31).

10. It is interesting that although the AACC clearly encourages dialogue with black Africans in diaspora, John Mbiti argues that African theology has nothing to do with black theology (Mbiti 1974). However, Mbiti's view represents a minority view among African theologians, as demonstrated by repeated theological dialogues among black theologians and African theologians. If African and black theologies have nothing to do with each other, why so many dialogues? Desmond Tutu, a South African, and James Cone, a black American, have challenged Mbiti's perspective on this issue. (See especially Cone 1979 and Tutu 1975.) Furthermore, the welcome and rewarding presence of black theologians at the Pan-African Conference at Ghana in December 1977 is another indication that Mbiti's perspective is accepted neither by Africans nor black Americans. Mshana (1972a) indicates that these two theologies enrich each other through dialogue.

11. The term *moratorium* is interpreted by African theologians and church leaders to mean the suspension of Euro-American missionaries and their funds from the African churches in order that the African church may "find itself" and set strategies for self-reliance. The chief spokespersons in the continent are John Gatu and Canon Burgess Carr. (See AACC 1975.) See also Burgess Carr's articles "The Moratorium: The Search for Self-Reliance and Authenticity" and "The Mission of the Moratorium" in *AACC Bulletin*. Also see the *International Review of Mission* 64, no. 254 (April 1975). The journal was titled "Moratorium?" and was entirely de-

voted to that subject. Note that this journal used to be known as the *International Review of Missions* (with an "s") but after a redefinition of "mission," it was decided that there can be only one mission of the church of Jesus Christ.

12. See *International Review of Mission* 65, no. 258 (April 1976).

13. AACC 1975, 17. Gatu gave a speech at the mission festival in Milwaukee in October 1971. Also, see the sermon he preached at the AACC assembly in Lusaka in 1974, entitled "For We Preach Not Ourselves, but Jesus Christ as Lord and Ourselves as Your Servants for Jesus' Sake" (2 Cor. 4:5).

14. Carr made speeches at the National Council of Churches in New York City. It is fair to say that he was the chief spokesperson on the subject. His position then as the general secretary of the AACC facilitated and necessitated his extensive involvement. He is a capable and eloquent theologian as well. Carr (a Liberian) is also one of the African exponents of a liberation theology. His views have been expressed in the *AACC Bulletin* as well as in other places, including *The Struggle Continues,* the official report of the third AACC assembly (AACC 1975).

15. A case in point is a top official within the Board of Global Ministries of the United Methodist Church in New York. When an African minister asked for funds to purchase a ticket to return to his home country after completing a doctoral degree, this official took the trouble to make reservations, not out of a spirit of service, but because he could not trust the African with a thousand dollars. When an African bishop came to the board to ask for funds to repair school and church buildings that had been destroyed during the liberation struggle in Zimbabwe, the board had to send envoys all the way to Africa to estimate the actual financial need and to decide whether the stated need was worth the "missionary dollars."

16. 1 Cor. 12:12–27 describes the church as the Body of Christ.

Chapter 6: The Theology of African Traditional Religion

1. See Mbiti 1976b; Fashole-Luke 1975; and Agbeti 1972, 5–8. These authors attempt to define the terms, but the issue has not been resolved.

2. For a written source of African traditional prayers see Mbiti 1975b and Shorter 1972.

3. This proverb sounds like Job 1:21. See Dickson 1979. This similarity between the Bible and aspects of African culture makes the Scriptures relevant to Africans almost naturally.

4. Manas Buthelezi makes this point. He contends that the true African is "the one we see in Johannesburg, Durban, Cape Town trying to make ends meet in the framework of Influx-Control legislation" (1978, 64).

5. In Zimbabwe there is a tree where travellers "stop in" for lunch or

supper provided by God under the tree. The tree is known today as the "tree without a name." It is located about 60 kilometers from Harare. This information came from my own research on African traditional religion.

6. Though Mbiti defines theology as a theological reflection by African Christians, his own method is descriptive. African theology seeks to combine these two in its formulations.

7. Mbiti's *Concepts of God in Africa* (1970b) is systematic.

8. Sergio Torres's "Opening Address" in *African Theology en Route* (Appiah-Kubi and Torres 1979, 3–9) discusses the importance of a new epistemology for a genuinely African theology. Sergio Torres is, of course, not talking about traditional theology.

9. Fred B. Craddock's *Pre-existence of Christ in the New Testament* (1968) is a detailed account of the concept of the preexistent Christ. This rather exhaustive work does not make any reference to African traditional religion.

Chapter 7: African Theology

1. Complete documentation of the works mentioned in this chapter may be found in the Bibliography.

2. See chapter 6 for a detailed account of terminology and its problems and for my point of view.

3. Although biblical revelation was to become a major source for the African theologians, in this early work only one chapter, on eschatology, is biblical.

4. The Conference of Black Churchmen was held in Tanzania from August 22 to 28, 1971. It was sponsored by the African Commission of the National Committee of Black Churchmen in the United States and the Tanzania Consultative Council. Their theme was "Black Identity and Solidarity and the Role of the Church as a Medium for Social Change." See Mshana 1972a, 19–30.

5. See chapter 4 on Pan-Africanism and African nationalism.

6. The theme was "Theological Consultation on African Theology and Church Life." The consultation was held from January 1 to 7, 1972. See Mshana 1972a, 19–30.

7. Articles written by African theologians since then demonstrate this interest. See, for example, Kallu 1974 and Appiah-Kubi 1974.

8. From the papers and discussions of this conference came a theological text: *The Emergent Gospel: Theology from the Underside of History* (Torres and Fabella 1978). Although the consultation was concerned about Third World theologies in general, specific articles relate to the development of an African theology. Manas Buthelezi's "Toward Indigenous

Theology in South Africa" (1978) and Charles Nyamiti's "Approaches to African Theology" (1978) are examples.

9. The conference was held in Accra, Ghana, from December 17 to 23, 1977. This was the first theological conference in which I participated. I was the only one who represented Zimbabwe although I was then at Union Theological Seminary in New York, where I was doing doctoral studies. The conference gave me a much broader and deeper perspective on the issues and problems involved in the creation of African theology.

10. I am not aware of other books on African theology at this time. It is this scarcity of textbooks on African theology that tends to make the subject a "ghost" for most people.

11. See the Bibliography for a list of Mbiti's articles.

12. See especially Dickson 1979, 95ff.

13. Appiah-Kubi questions the all-embracing term *African Christian theology*. He offers a working label: *Contextual African Biblical Theology*. See Appiah-Kubi 1974, 6.

14. See Sawyerr 1964. *The Ghana Bulletin of Theology* 4 (Dec. 1971) has four articles on sin.

15. AACC 1970, 115. I have italicized *Christian* for emphasis.

Chapter 8: Black Theology in South Africa

1. Basil Moore explains that the term *black theology* spilled over from the United States, but the content of black theology in South Africa is unique for that situation. See Moore 1974, 1.

2. This book contains essays that define black theology in its South African context.

3. Allan Boesak is a young black theologian in South Africa, an ordained minister of the Dutch Reformed Church. His contribution is making an impact on both black and African theologians.

4. See note 1 above.

5. Sundkler 1961, 40. This is discussed in chapter 3.

6. For this reason Buthelezi rejects African traditional religious background and culture as the basis for an African theology. See Buthelezi 1978, 62.

7. It was the same year that black North Americans "affirmed the Black Power statement and derived from it a theological analysis that sets the stage for the emergence of Black theology" (Wilmore and Cone 1979, 15).

8. George Mukgethi Motlhabi edited *Essays in Black Theology* (Johannesburg, 1972). The American edition is entitled *The Challenge of Black Theology in South Africa* and was edited by Basil Moore (1974).

9. In his book, he notes: "Although some black theologians, especially in North America, have made 'blackness' into some kind of basic criterion for Christian faith and action, this is certainly not true of black theology in South Africa. Allan Boesak has made this quite clear in his criticism of James Cone. For Boesak . . . 'black' has to do with the existential situation, not with the criterion of theology" (de Gruchy 1979, 159).

10. John Mbiti is one. He warns that if biblical backing is lacking in liberation theology, ". . . that branch of African theology will lose its credibility" (1979, 89).

11. See Tutu 1975. I do not wish to go into the debate on whether the two theologies are "soul mates" or "antagonists." My purpose here is only to describe the origin and development of African theology.

12. See Mbiti 1974, 43. Note that reference is made to North American black theology of which South African black theology is an offshoot. It might be inconsistent to affirm the one and condemn the other.

13. The previous chapter which discussed African Christian theology has demonstrated where its emphasis is.

14. George Thomas as quoted by Mshana (1972a, 23).

Suggested Readings

Many books and articles have contributed to the origin and development of African theology. Rather than discuss the contributions chronologically, I prefer to discuss them topically, roughly corresponding to their appearance in the text.

According to John S. Mbiti, a generally respected authority in African theology, the term *African theology* first appeared in 1956 (Fueter 1956). This date marks the beginnings of a distinctively African theology for most African theologians. Consequently the sources of African theology I discuss here come after 1956, except for some germane sources that precede this date.

African Traditional Religion

African theology draws heavily on African traditional religion. Therefore there has been great interest in works on African traditional religion. Major works include Edwin Smith's book entitled, *African Ideas of God* (1950). This book makes a special contribution on the traditional ideas of God, which African theologians are attempting to systematize into a more or less coherent doctrine of God. Geoffrey E. Parrinder has written two books, *African Traditional Religion* (1957) and *Religion in Africa* (1969). The former places emphasis on traditional religion. The latter treats not only African traditional religion but other religions in Africa as well. D. Forde's *African Worlds* (1954) on African cosmology in general is important.

Van der Merwe did a localized study of the Shona (my own tribe) and wrote *The Shona Idea of God* (1957). This booklet deals with God cults among the Shona. Another work that is very useful is the book resulting from a symposium on various aspects of African life and thought, *African Systems of Thought* (Fortes and Dieterlen 1965).

It is interesting to note that most of these books on African traditional life and thought were written by white people who, for some reason, took a keen interest in the African traditional religious background, although it had been condemned by the white missionaries as ungodly. It is worth noting that most of these European authors approached the subject from the point of view of anthropology, rather than theology.

African writers emerged in the sixties. It was also during the sixties that most states achieved their political independence. The All Africa Conference of Churches (AACC), a body intended to be independent of the overseas boards and agencies, also emerged during the sixties. It is fair to say Africa was finding itself and was ready to speak for itself. This was also the time when articles and books on African theology began to appear. Evidently the political spirit greatly influenced the spiritual institutions.

John S. Mbiti has written several books, most of which pertain to African traditional religion. The first one, *African Religions and Philosophy* (1970a), won him his present reputation. He also wrote *Concepts of God in Africa* (1970b), which focuses on the African concepts of God, and *Introduction to African Religion* (1975a), which touches on all aspects of traditional life and thought. *The Prayers of African Religion* (1975b) is an anthology of African traditional prayers. All these books are very useful sources for African theology. For more works by Mbiti, I refer the reader to the Bibliography.

E. Bolaji Idowu wrote *African Traditional Religion: A Definition* (1975). This is one of the most useful texts on the subject. It also serves to correct some of the erroneous theories about African traditional religion. Harry Sawyerr's *God: Ancestor or Creator* (1970) focuses on a central theme, namely God and the ancestors. Sawyerr attempts to define the African concept of God, as do other African writers on the subject. For more works, see the Bibliography.

We might add here that when African authors came on board, the content of African traditional religion acquired an indigenous aura. However, as was the case with most European authors, Christian influence often tended to distort a proper perspective of African traditional religion in these books. Traditional religion tended to be presented in the light of Christianity, and not in its own right. Nevertheless, we are still thankful for these descriptive accounts of traditional religion. They provide African theologians with a framework within which to develop African theologies.

Malcolm J. McVeigh's *God in Africa* (1974a) is a systematic attempt to deal with Edwin Smith's descriptive works on the African's idea of God and religion in general. Since McVeigh is an American missionary, we can appreciate the work's Christian bias. Michael Gelfand wrote *The Spiritual Beliefs of the Shona* (1977). This book is of special interest to me because it attempts to describe my cultural and spiritual beliefs from the point of view of the African. It is also a thorough case study of the Shona's spiritual beliefs.

These books do not deal exclusively with the theology of African traditional religion. They touch, at a descriptive level, upon topics in African traditional religion which inform African scholars in their endeavor to construct an African theology—topics such as ancestor, spirit, God, good and evil, and humanity. It is in this sense that we regard these books as part of our African theological heritage.

I contend that African theology is embedded in these works. This is demonstrated in chapter 1 where we dealt with African traditional religion and the origin of African theology. The Bible and the Christian tradition are also regarded as sources of African theology by many African theologians.

Christianity in Africa

Several books have been written on Christianity in Africa or African Christianity. Most of these books juxtapose Christianity and African religion and culture. The African theologian makes the best use of the tension implied between the Christian faith and African life and thought. Used this way, these books serve as the raw material for an African theological heritage.

Bengt G. Sundkler's book entitled *The Christian Ministry in Africa* (1960) made a real impact in Africa. It certainly prepared the church for the emergence of African theology, although the book itself is not a text on African theology.

Harry Sawyerr wrote *Creative Evangelism: Towards a New Christian Encounter with Africa* (1968). Again the tension between Christianity and culture is brought to bear. Christiansen G. Baeta edited *Christianity in Tropical Africa* (1968), a book that consists of scholarly essays by experts in their field. G. C. Oosthuizen wrote *Post-Christianity in Africa* (1968), which tells the story of African independency at the same time that it discusses Christianity in Africa. These three books are by African scholars who discuss Christianity in Africa as they perceive it.

T. A. Beetham's *Christianity and the New Africa* (1967) gives a historical perspective of Christianity in Africa, that is, the planting of the Christian faith and the African response. This book provides the African theologian with very rich raw material for the development of African theology.

There are three edited volumes which bring together a diversity of scholarship on African Christianity. *A New Look at Christianity in Africa* (World Student Christian Federation 1970) juxtaposes Christianity and African culture and beliefs. J. A. Dachs (1973) edited *Christianity South of the Zambezi* (vol. 1). M. F. C. Bourdillon (1977) edited *Christianity South of the Zambezi* (vol. 2). Both books consist of articles on the planting of Christianity in Africa and the African response. That is vital material for African theology.

Aylward Shorter has written several books on Christianity and African culture from the point of view of an anthropologist who is also a priest. He wrote *African Culture and the Christian Church* (1974) and edited *African Christian Spirituality* (1978). Since both books provide the African theologian with raw materials for African theology, I consider them as part of the African theological heritage.

Books by Adrian Hastings serve as sources for church history as well as African theology. He authored *African Christianity* (1977) and *A History of African Christianity 1950–1975* (1979), which is a systematic presentation of the events in the historic church, the state, and independency. Other authors have devoted whole volumes to the African indigenous Christian churches and discussed them both individually and collectively.

The African Indigenous Churches

Because the African indigenous church movement is considered to be one of the major sources for African theology, books on aspects of the movement should be treated as the raw material for the African theological heritage.

Bengt G. Sundkler's *Bantu Prophets in South Africa* (1961) is an excellent treatment of the rise of independency in South Africa. Martin Daneel wrote two books, *Old and New in Southern Shona Independent Churches* (1974) and *Zionism and Faith-Healing in Rhodesia* (1970). Both focus on a particular region in Zimbabwe in order to produce fine details which are needed in doing African theology.

David Barrett's *Schism and Renewal in Africa* (1968) is the most comprehensive work on the African independent churches so far. The author actually indicates that African theology should develop from the many aspects and themes raised in the independent church movement. A. Hastings's *A History of African Christianity 1950–1975* (1979) also covers a span of independency but not nearly as thoroughly as Barrett's *Schism and Renewal in Africa*.

Prophetism in Ghana by Christiansen Baeta (1962) is also a regional study of independency with special attention to the "spirit churches." G. Halliburton's *The Prophet Harris* (1971) gives an account of William Wadé Harris's rise to evangelistic fame and his influence and impact on the African people at the beginning of this century. It compares well with the story of the prophet Simon Kimbangu's rise to spiritual fame and his consequent influence and impact among the African people.

So far we have discussed materials that impact more or less indirectly upon the theological heritage of Africa. Now we indicate the materials that impact directly upon the African theological heritage.

African Nationalism

Sources on African nationalism and Pan-Africanism discuss not only African movements on the continent but also in the diaspora. Among them are works by W. E. B. DuBois, notably *The World and Africa* (1965), and Marcus Garvey's *Africa for Africans* (Jacques-Garvey [1923-26] 1967). Immanuel Geiss's *The Pan-African Movement* (1974) is one of the best documents available. S. A. Akintoye wrote *Emergent African States* (1976). It focuses on the African states. The Rev. N. Sithole authored *African Nationalism* (1954), which deals mostly with nationalist activities with reference to the author's own nation of Zimbabwe. These sources provide us with a background against which African theology is being developed. They have also made a significant impact and influence on the church in Africa.

The All Africa Conference of Churches

The All Africa Conference of Churches (AACC) is an important source of African theology. Therefore all the published reports of the assembly are of vital importance for our purpose here. Notable are *The Drumbeats from Kampala* (1963), *Engagement: Abidjan 1969* (1970), and *The Struggle Continues* (1975). Most of the volumes of the *AACC Bulletins* are also invaluable. The AACC is discussed in chapter 5.

African Theologies

There is plethora of articles on African theology or African Christian theology (I explain the distinction between these terms in chapters 5 and 6), but only a few books on the subject.

Aylward Shorter wrote *African Christian Theology: Adaptation or Incarnation* (1977). It is a highly systematized study on religion and philosophy in Africa. The book encourages African theologians to do African theology more than it actually develops a theology itself. The second assembly of the All Africa Conference of Churches' set out guidelines for African theology in its official report *Engagement: Abidjan 1969* (1970).

In 1975 Byang H. Kato wrote *Theological Pitfalls in Africa* (1975), a critique of African theology. The Pan-African Conference of Third World Theologians has made a theological contribution to the development of

African theology with *African Theology en Route*, edited by Kofi Appiah-Kubi and Sergio Torres (1979). The first consultation had been held in Dar es Salaam. Sergio Torres and Virginia Fabella (1978) edited the articles and produced *The Emergent Gospel*. Both books are important to the African theological heritage because they come out of a group's conscious effort to create African theology. In addition, there are individuals who have written books on the subject.

John S. Pobee wrote *Toward an African Theology* (1979). This is an attempt by an individual to make a theological statement on various theological themes such as evil, christology, marriage, and so forth. Pobee also attempts to define African theology.

Kwesi Dickson and Paul Ellingworth edited *Biblical Revelation and African Beliefs* (1971). This book was a result of a joint effort by two African theologians, sponsored by the All Africa Conference of Churches, to get a theological text that would set a good example of what direction African theology ought to take. Mbiti edited *African and Asian Contributions to Contemporary Theology: Report* (1976a), which carries articles on the theologies of the two continents.

From South Africa there are three books on black theology. Basil Moore edited *The Challenge of Black Theology in South Africa* (1974). This volume is the cornerstone of South African black theology. Allan Boesak wrote *Farewell to Innocence: A Socio-Ethical Study on Black Theology and Power* (1977), which discusses North American and South African black theologies. Gayraud Wilmore and James H. Cone (1979) coauthored and edited *Black Theology: A Documentary History 1966–1979*. We must consider this as a part of the African heritage because the discussion on black theology and African theology done there is not available anywhere else in "African" literature. The authors' perspective is significant for us since it places African theology in a global context.

Many articles on African theology (and there are many) are included in the bibliography of this work. They are discussed in the body of the text in relation to their importance to the development of African theology.

Bibliography

AACC. 1963. *The Drumbeats from Kampala*. London: Lutterworth Press.
———. 1970. *Engagement: Abidjan 1969*. Nairobi.
———. 1975. *The Struggle Continues*. Nairobi.
AACC Bulletin 8, no. 3.
Agbeti, John K. 1972. "African Theology: What It Is." *Presence* 5:5–8.
Akintoye, S. A. 1976. *Emergent African States: Topics in Twentieth Century African History*. London: Longman Group.
Anderson, Gerald. 1961. *The Theology of the Christian Mission*. New York: McGraw Hill.
———. 1974. "A Moratorium on Missionaries?" In *Mission Trends No. 1*, edited by Gerald H. Anderson and Thomas F. Stransky, 133–141. New York: Paulist Press.
Anderson, Gerald H., and Thomas F. Stransky, eds. 1974. *Mission Trends No. 1*. New York: Paulist Press.
———. 1976. *Mission Trends No. 3: Third World Theologies*. New York: Paulist Press.
———. 1979. *Mission Trends No. 4: Liberation Theologies*. New York: Paulist Press.
Appiah-Kubi, Kofi. 1974. "Why African Theology?" *AACC Bulletin* 7.
———. 1975. "The Church's Healing Ministry in Africa." *The Ecumenical Review* 27:230–239.
———. 1977. "Jesus Christ: Some Christological Aspects from African Perspectives." In *African and Asian Contributions to Contemporary Theology: Report,* edited by John Mbiti, 51–65. Geneva: Bossey.
———. 1979. "Indigenous African Christian Churches: Signs of Authenticity." In *African Theology en Route,* edited by Kofi Appiah-Kubi and Sergio Torres, 117–125. Maryknoll, N.Y.: Orbis Books.
Appiah-Kubi, Kofi, and Sergio Torres, eds. 1979. *African Theology en Route*. Maryknoll, N.Y.: Orbis Books.
Baeta, C. G. 1962. *Prophetism in Ghana*. London: S.C.M. Press.

Baeta, C. G., ed. 1968. *Christianity in Tropical Africa: Studies Presented and Discussed at the International African Seminar,* University of Ghana, April 1965. London: Oxford University Press.

Barrett, David. 1968. *Schism and Renewal in Africa.* London: Oxford University Press.

———. 1971. *African Initiatives in Religion.* Nairobi: East African Publishing House.

Beetham, T. A. 1967. *Christianity and the New Africa.* New York: Frederick A. Praeger.

Bhebe, N. M. B. 1973. "Missionary Activity among the Ndebele and Kalanga: A Survey." In *Christianity South of the Zambezi,* vol. 1, edited by Anthony J. Dachs. Gwelo: Mambo Press.

Bienen, Henry. 1974. *Kenya: The Politics of Participation and Control.* Princeton: Princeton University Press.

Bigo, Pierre. 1977. *The Church and Third World Revolutions.* Maryknoll, N.Y.: Orbis Books.

Boesak, Allan. 1977. *Farewell to Innocence: A Socio-Ethical Study on Black Theology and Power.* Maryknoll, N.Y.: Orbis Books.

———. 1978. "Coming in out of the Wilderness." In *The Emergent Gospel,* edited by S. Torres and V. Fabella. Maryknoll, N.Y.: Orbis Books.

———. 1979. "Liberation Theology in South Africa." In *African Theology en Route,* edited by Kofi Appiah-Kubi and Sergio Torres, 169–75. Maryknoll, N.Y.: Orbis Books.

Boff, Leonardo. 1978. *Jesus Christ Liberator: A Critical Christology for Our Time.* Maryknoll, N.Y.: Orbis Books.

Booth, Newell S., ed. 1977. *African Religions: A Symposium.* New York: NOK Publishers.

Bourdillon, M. F. C., ed. 1977. *Christianity South of the Zambezi.* Vol. 2. Gwelo: Mambo Press.

Braaten, Carl E. 1975. "Christian Mission and American Imperialism." *Dialog* 15:70–78.

Buthelezi, Manas. 1973. "African Theology and Black Theology: A Search for Theological Method." In *Relevant Theology for Africa,* edited by H. J. Becken, 20ff. Durban: Lutheran Publishing House.

———. 1974a. "An African Theology or Black Theology?" In *The Challenge of Black Theology in South Africa,* edited by Basil Moore, 29–35. Atlanta: John Knox.

———. 1974b. "The Theological Meaning of True Humanity." In ibid., 93–103.

———. 1978. "Toward Indigenous Theology in South Africa." In *The Emergent Gospel,* edited by Sergio Torres and Virginia Fabella, 56–75. Maryknoll, N.Y.: Orbis Books.

Camus, Albert. 1956. *The Rebel.* New York: Vintage Books.

Carr, Burgess. 1972a. "A Report to the Executive Committee of the AACC." Document no. 1 (March 1972).

———. 1972b. "A Letter to the Heads of Governments in Africa." *The Hard Road to Peace* (April 4, 1972).

———. 1974. "The Moratorium: The Search for Self-Reliance and Authenticity." *AACC Bulletin* 7 (May/June).

———. 1975. "The Mission of the Moratorium." *AACC Bulletin* 8:21-24.

———. n.d.(a). "Internationalizing the Mission." Mimeo.

———. n.d.(b). "A Report to the Executive Committee of the Division of Overseas Ministries, U.S. Council of Churches: 'The Mission of the Moratorium.' "

Cartey, Wilfred, and Martin Kilson, eds. 1970. *The African Reader: Colonial Africa* (African reaction and adaptation, emergence of masses, formation of national institutions). New York: Vintage Books.

Chasanga, J., and Dr. W. Wille, trans. 1973. "No, There Is No Problem between God, Mobutu and Zaireans." *National Daily* (Kinshasa, April 14-15, 1973.)

Chennells, A. 1973. "The Image of the Ndebele and the Nineteenth Century Missionary Tradition." In *Christianity South of the Zambezi,* edited by Anthony J. Dachs. Gwelo: Mambo Press.

Coggins, W. T. 1974. "What's Behind the Idea of Missionary Moratorium?" *Christianity Today* 19 (Nov. 22, 1974): 7-9.

Coleman, J. S. 1958. *Nigeria: A Background to Nationalism.* Berkeley: University of California Press.

Cone, James H. 1969. *Black Theology and Black Power.* New York: Seabury Press.

———. 1970. *A Black Theology of Liberation.* Philadelphia: Lippincott.

———. 1973. "Black Theology on Revolution, Violence and Reconciliation." *Dialogue* 12 (Spring 1973): 127-133.

———. 1975a. "Black and African Theologies: A Consultation." *Christianity and Crisis* 35 (March 3, 1975): 50-52.

———. 1975b. *God of the Oppressed.* New York: Seabury Press.

———. 1979. "A Black American Perspective of the Future of African Theology." In *African Theology en Route,* edited by Kofi Appiah-Kubi and Sergio Torres, 176-186. Maryknoll, N.Y.: Orbis Books.

Craddock, Fred B. 1968. *Pre-existence of Christ in the New Testament.* Nashville: Abingdon Press.

Cronon, E. David. 1969. *Black Moses: The Story of Marcus Garvey and the Universal Negro Improvement Association.* 2nd ed. Madison, Wis.: University of Wisconsin Press.

Dachs, Anthony J., ed. 1973. *Christianity South of the Zambezi,* vol. 1. Gwelo: Mambo Press.

Daneel, M. L. 1970. *Zionism and Faith-Healing in Rhodesia: Aspects of African Independent Churches.* The Hague: Mouton.

————. 1974. *Old and New in Southern Shona Independent Churches.* Vol. 2. The Hague: Mouton.

Davidson, Basil. 1968. *Africa in History: Themes and Outlines.* London: Weidenfeld and Nicolson.

————. 1978. *Let Freedom Come: Africa in Modern History.* Boston: Little, Brown and Co.

de Gruchy, John W. 1979. *The Church Struggle in South Africa.* Grand Rapids, Mich.: Eerdmans.

Dickson, Kwesi A. 1973. "The Old Testament and African Theology." *The Ghana Bulletin of Theology* 4 (June 1973): 31ff.

————. 1974. "Towards a Theologia Africana." In *New Testament Christianity for Africa and the World,* edited by M. E. Glasswell and E. W. Fashole-Luke, 198–208. London: S.P.C.K.

————. 1979. "Continuity and Discontinuity between the Old Testament and African Life and Thought." In *African Theology en Route,* edited by K. Appiah-Kubi and S. Torres, 95–108. Maryknoll, N.Y.: Orbis Books.

Dickson, Kwesi A., and Paul Ellingworth, eds. 1971. *Biblical Revelation and African Beliefs.* Maryknoll, N.Y.: Orbis Books.

Dillenberger, John, and Claude Welch, eds. 1954. *Protestant Christianity.* New York: Charles Scribner's Sons.

DuBois, W. E. B. 1965. *The World and Africa: An Inquiry into the Part Which Africa Has Played in World History.* New York: International Publishers.

Evans-Pritchard, E. E. 1956. *Nuer Religion.* London: Oxford University Press.

Fabella, Virginia, ed. 1980. *Asia's Struggle for Full Humanity: Towards a Relevant Theology.* Maryknoll, N.Y.: Orbis Books.

Fashole-Luke, E. W. 1974. "Ancestor Veneration and the Communion of Saints." In *New Testament Christianity for Africa and the World,* edited by Mark E. Glasswell and Edward W. Fashole-Luke. London: S.P.C.K.

————. 1975. "The Quest for an African Christian Theology." *The Ecumenical Review* 27 (July 1975): 259–69.

————. 1981. "Footpaths and Signposts to African Christian Theologies." *Bulletin of African Theology* 3 (Jan.–June 1981): 19–40.

Ferkiss, Victor C. 1966. *Africa's Search for Identity.* New York: The World Publishing Co.

Feuerbach, Ludwig. 1957. *The Essence of Christianity.* New York: Harper & Row.

Forde, Daryll. 1954. *African Worlds: Studies in the Cosmological Ideas and Social Values of African Peoples.* Oxford: Oxford University Press.

Fortes, M., and G. Dieterlen. 1965. *African Systems of Thought* (Studies presented and discussed at the Third International Seminar in Salisbury, December 1960). London: Oxford University Press.

Fueter, P. D. 1956. "Theological Education in Africa." *International Review of Missions* 27 (Geneva).

Geiss, Immanuel. 1974. *The Pan-African Movement: A History of Pan-Africanism in America, Europe and Africa.* New York: Holmes and Meier.

Gelfand, Michael. 1973. *The Genuine Shona: Survival Values of an African Culture.* Gwelo: Mambo Press.

———. 1977. *The Spiritual Beliefs of the Shona.* Gwelo: Mambo Press.

Gelzer, David G. 1970. "Random Notes on Black Theology and African Theology." *Christian Century* 87 (Sept. 1970): 1091–1093.

Gibson, Richard. 1972. *African Liberation Movements: Contemporary Struggles Against White Minority Rule.* London: Oxford University Press.

Glasswell, Mark E., and E. W. Fashole-Luke, eds. 1974. *New Testament Christianity for Africa and the World: Essays in Honor of Harry Sawyerr.* London: S.P.C.K.

Greaves, L. B. 1958. "The All Africa Church Conference: Ibadan, Nigeria, 10th to 20th January 1958." *The International Review of Missions:* 257–263.

Gutiérrez, Gustavo. 1973. *A Theology of Liberation: History, Politics and Salvation.* Maryknoll, N.Y.: Orbis Books.

Gutkind, Peter, and Peter Waterman, eds. 1977. *African Social Studies: A Radical Reader.* New York: Monthly Review Press.

Halliburton, G. 1971. *The Prophet Harris.* Harlow: Longman.

Hamutyinei, M. A., and A. B. Plangger, eds. 1974. *Tsumo-Shumo: Shona Proverbial Lore and Wisdom.* Gwelo: Mambo Press.

Hastings, Adrian. 1977. *African Christianity.* New York: Seabury Press.

———. 1979. *A History of African Christianity 1950–1975.* Cambridge: Cambridge University Press.

Hayward, Victor E. W. 1963. *African Independent Church Movements.* London: Edinburgh House Press.

Hodgkin, T. 1956. *Nationalism in Colonial Africa.* London: Muller.

Hollenwager, Walter J. 1974. *Pentecost Between Black and White: Five Case Studies on Pentecost and Politics.* Belfast: Christian Journals.

Hooker, J. R. 1967. *Black Revolutionary: George Padmore's Path from Communism to Pan-Africanism.* London: London University Press.

Hull, Richard. 1980. *Modern Africa: Change and Continuity.* Englewood Cliffs, N.J.: Prentice-Hall.

Idowu, E. Bolaji. 1962. *Olodumare: God in Yoruba Belief.* London: Oxford University Press.

————. 1965. *Towards an Indigenous Church.* London: Oxford University Press.

————. 1975. *African Traditional Religion: A Definition.* Maryknoll, N.Y.: Orbis Books.

Ilogu, Edmund. 1970. "Independent African Churches in Nigeria." *International Review of Missions* (Jan./Oct.): 492–97.

Jacques-Garvey, Amy, ed. (1923–26) 1967. *Philosophy and Opinions of Marcus Garvey* or *Africa for the Africans.* 2 vols. Edited by E. U. Essien-Udom (London). New York: Arno Press.

Journal of an Expedition up the Niger and Tshadda Rivers. 1855. London: Church Missionary House.

July, Robert W. 1970. *A History of the African People.* New York: Charles Scribner's Sons.

Kahler, Martin. 1964. *The So-called Historical Jesus and the Biblical Christ.* Philadelphia: Fortress Press.

Kalilombe, P. A. 1979. "Self-Reliance of the African Church: A Catholic Perspective." In *African Theology en Route,* edited by Kofi Appiah-Kubi and Sergio Torres, 36–58. Maryknoll, N.Y.: Orbis Books.

Kallu, Henry. 1974. "Africa: What Kind of Theology?" *AACC Bulletin* 7 (Jan./Feb.).

Kappen, Sebastian. 1977. *Jesus and Freedom.* Maryknoll, N.Y.: Orbis Books.

Kaseman, Ernst. 1970. *Jesus Means Freedom.* Philadelphia: Fortress Press.

Kato, Byang H. 1975. *Theological Pitfalls in Africa.* Kisumu: Evangel Publishing House.

Kaufmann, L. 1973. "Theological Education in the 1970's" *African Ecclesiastical Review* 15 (July 3, 1973).

Kennedy, James. 1976. *Nairobi: A First Hand Report of the Fifth Assembly of the World Council of Churches.* Cincinnati: Forward Movement Publications.

Kibichu, Samuel. 1970. "African Traditional Religion and Christianity." In *A New Look at Christianity in Africa.* Vol. 2, no. 2. Geneva: WSCF Books.

Koyama, Kosuke. 1974. "What Makes a Missionary? Toward a Crucified

Mind, Not a Crusading Mind." In *Mission Trends No. 1,* edited by G. H. Anderson and T. F. Stransky, 117–132. New York: Paulist Press.

Kurewa, John. 1975. "The Meaning of African Theology." *Journal of Theology for Southern Africa* 11:32–42.

———. 1976. "An African Perspective of Jesus Christ." A paper presented to the Africa Central Conference Meeting at Mindola Ecumenical Institute, Kitwe, Zambia, August 16–22, 1976.

La Guma, Alex. 1971. *Apartheid: A Collection of Writings on South African Racism by South Africans.* New York: International Publishers.

Lewis, Warren, ed. 1978. *Towards a Global Congress of World Religions.* New York: The Rose of Sharon Press.

Lloyd, Peter. 1967. *Africa in Social Change.* London: Cox and Wyman.

Long, Charles. 1975. "Structural Similarities and Dissimilarities." *Journal of Religious Thought* 33 (Fall/Winter 1975): 9–24.

Lugira, A. M. n.d. *Africa Theological Journal* 5:53ff.

McVeigh, Malcolm J. 1974a. *God in Africa: Conceptions of God in African Traditional Religion and Christianity.* Cape Cod: Claude Stark.

———. 1974b. "Sources for an African Christian Theology." *Presence 5.*

Mack, R. 1975. "Basic Aspects of Revelation in the Old Testament." *The Ghana Bulletin of Theology* 448 (June 1975): 13–23.

Macquarrie, John. 1966. *Principles of Christian Theology.* 2nd ed. New York: Charles Scribner's Sons.

Martin, Marie-Louise. 1975. *Kimbangu: An African Prophet and His Church.* Oxford: Basil Blackwell.

Massie, P., ed. 1973. *Black Faith and Solidarity.* New York: Friendship Press.

Maveneka, Alois. 1978. *A Church Self-Reliant and Missionary.* Gwelo: Mambo Press.

Mbiti, John S. 1968. "Ways and Means of Communicating the Gospel." In *Christianity in Tropical Africa,* edited by C. G. Baeta, 329–350. London: Oxford University Press.

———. 1970a. *African Religions and Philosophy.* New York: Doubleday.

———. 1970b. *Concepts of God in Africa.* London: S.P.C.K.

———. 1972a. "Church and State: A Neglected Element of Christianity." *Africa Journal of Theology* 5 (December 1972).

———. 1972b. *New Testament Eschatology in an African Background.* London: Oxford University Press.

———. 1972c. "Some African Concepts of Christology." In *Christ and the Younger Churches,* edited by G. F. Vicedom, 51ff. London: S.P.C.K.

——. 1973a. "African Theology." *Worldview* (August 1973): 33–39.

——. 1973b. "Salvation as an African Experience." In *Christ and Spirit in the New Testament,* edited by B. Linars and S. S. Smalley. London: The University Press.

——. 1974. "An African Views American Black Theology." *Worldview* (August 1974): 42ff.

——. 1975a. *Introduction to African Religion.* New York: Praeger Publishers.

——. 1975b. *The Prayers of African Religion.* Maryknoll, N.Y.: Orbis Books.

Mbiti, John S., ed. 1976a. *African and Asian Contributions to Contemporary Theology: Report.* Geneva: Bossey.

Mbiti, John S. 1976b. "Some Currents of African Theology." In *African and Asian Contributions to Contemporary Theology: Report,* edited by John S. Mbiti, 6–17. Geneva: Bossey.

——. 1978a. "African Theology." In *All Africa Lutheran Consultation on Theology in the African Context* (Oct. 5–14, 1978): 33ff.

——. 1978b. "Cattle Are Born with Ears, Their Horns Will Grow Later: Towards an Appreciation of African Oral Theology." *Africa Journal of Theology* 5.

——. 1979a. "The Biblical Basis for the Present Trends in African Theology." In *African Theology en Route,* edited by Kofi Appiah-Kubi and Sergio Torres, 83–94. Maryknoll, N.Y.: Orbis Books.

——. 1979b. "Experience and Theology, A Report of Group 4 at a Theological Colloquium in Geneva." In *Indigenous Theology and the Universal Church,* edited by John S. Mbiti. Geneva: Bossey.

——. 1980. "The Encounter of Christian Faith and African Religion." *The Christian Century* (Aug. 27, 1980): 817–820.

Mgojo. 1973. "Prolegomenon to the Study of Black Theology." *Journal of Theology for Southern Africa* 21 (Dec. 1973): 28ff.

Monk, William, ed. 1918. *Dr. Livingstone's Cambridge Lectures.* Cambridge: Cambridge University Press.

Moore, Basil, ed. 1973. *Black Theology: The South African Voice.* London: Hurst and Co.

Moore, Basil. 1974. *The Challenge of Black Theology in South Africa.* Atlanta: John Knox Press.

Mosha, Raymond. 1980. "The Trinity in the African Context." *Africa Theological Journal* 9 (April 1980): 40–47.

Mshana, E. E. 1968. "Nationalism in Africa, as a Challenge and Problem." *Africa Theological Journal* 1 (Feb. 1968): 21–29.

——. 1972a. "The Challenge of Black Theology and African Theology." *Africa Theological Journal* 5 (Dec. 1972): 19–30.

———. 1972b. "Church and State in the Independent States of Africa." *Africa Theological Journal* 5 (Dec. 1972): 31–45.

Muzorewa, A. T. 1978. *Rise Up and Walk: An Autobiography.* Nashville: Abingdon.

Nacpil, Emerito P., and Douglas J. Elwood, eds. 1980. *The Human and the Holy: Asian Perspectives in Christian Theology.* Maryknoll, N.Y.: Orbis Books.

Ngally, J. 1975. "Jesus Christ and Liberation: A Bible Study." *The Ecumenical Review* 27 (July): 213–219.

Niebuhr, H. Richard. 1951. *Christ and Culture.* New York: Harper and Row.

Nkrumah, Kwame. 1961. *I Speak of Freedom: A Statement of African Ideology.* New York: Praeger.

———. 1962. *Towards Colonial Freedom.* London: Heinemann.

———. 1963. *Africa Must Unite.* London: Oxford University Press.

———. 1965. *Neo-Colonialism: The Last Stage of Imperialism.* New York: International Publishers.

———. 1970a. *Class Struggle in Africa.* New York: International Publishers.

———. 1970b. *Consciencism: Philosophy and Ideology for Decolonization.* New York: Monthly Review Press.

———. 1975. *Ghana: The Autobiography of Kwame Nkrumah.* New York: International Publishers.

Nolan, Albert. 1976. *Jesus before Christianity: The Gospel of Liberation.* Cape Town: David Philip.

Nyamiti, Charles. 1978. "Approaches to African Theology." In *The Emergent Gospel,* edited by Sergio Torres and Virginia Fabella, 33–45. Maryknoll, N.Y.: Orbis Books.

Nyerere, Julius. 1967. *Freedom and Unity.* Oxford: Oxford University Press.

———. 1968. *Ujamaa: Essays on Socialism.* Oxford: Oxford University Press.

Oduyoye, Mercy A. 1979. "The Value of African Religious Beliefs and Practices for Christian Theology." In *African Theology en Route,* edited by Kofi Appiah-Kubi and Sergio Torres. Maryknoll, N.Y.: Orbis Books.

Omoyajowo, Joseph A. 1972. "Christian Expression in African Indigenous Churches." *Presence* 5, no. 3.

———. 1973–1975. "Human Dignity and Personal Rites and Sacrifices in African Traditional Religion." *Journal of Religious Thought* 30–31.

Oosthuizen, G. C. 1968. *Post-Christianity in Africa: A Theological and Anthropological Study.* London: C. Hurst.

Parrinder, Geoffrey. 1954. *African Traditional Religion.* 3rd ed. London: Sheldon Press.

———. 1969. *Religion in Africa.* Penguin African Library.

Peel, J. D. Y. 1968. *Aladura: A Religious Movement among the Yoruba.* London: Oxford University Press.

Pobee, John S. 1973. "Theology." *The Ghana Bulletin of Theology* 4 (June): 1–13.

———. 1977. "Revelation in Jesus Christ and Experience of Faith in the African Church." A paper presented at Accra, Ghana, Dec. 17–23.

———. 1979. *Toward an African Theology.* Nashville: Abingdon.

Potholm, Christian P. 1976a. *Liberation and Exploitation: The Struggle for Ethiopia.* Washington, D.C.: University Press of America.

———. 1976b. *The Theory and Practice of African Politics.* Englewood Cliffs: Prentice-Hall.

Price, T. 1968. "The Missionary Struggle with Complexity." In *Christianity in Tropical Africa,* edited by C. G. Baeta. London: Oxford University Press.

Roberts, Deotis J. 1974. *A Black Political Theology.* Philadelphia: Westminster Press.

Rodney, Walter. 1974. *How Europe Underdeveloped Africa.* Washington, D.C.: Howard University Press.

Sarpong, Peter. 1975a. "Media of Revelation in African Traditional Religions." *The Ghana Bulletin of Theology* 4 (June): 40–47.

———. 1975b. "Christianity Should Be Africanized, Not to Africanize Christianity." *Africa Ecclesiastical Review* (Winter).

———. n.d. "Christianity and Traditional African Religion." *African Challenge.*

Sawyerr, Harry. 1963. "The Basis of a Theology for Africa." *International Review of Missions:* 266–278.

———. 1964. "Sin and Forgiveness in Africa." *Frontier* 7 (London): 60–63.

———. 1966. "Ancestor Worship II: The Rationale." *Sierra Leone Bulletin of Religion* 8:33–39.

———. 1968. *Creative Evangelism: Towards a New Christian Encounter with Africa.* London: Lutterworth Press.

———. 1970. *God: Ancestor or Creator?* London: Longman.

———. 1971a. "What Is African Christian Theology?" *Africa Theological Journal* 4.

———. 1971b. "What Is African Theology? A Case for Theologica Africana." *Africa Theological Journal* 4.

———. 1972. "Salvation Viewed from the African Situation." *Presence* 5, no. 3:16–23.

Seligman, C. G. 1966. *Races of Africa*. London: Oxford University Press.
Setiloane, Gabriel M. 1975. "Confessing Christ Today: From One African Perspective: Man in Community." *Journal of Theology for Southern Africa* 12 (September): 29–38.
———. 1976a. "I Am an African." In *Mission Trends No. 3: Third World Theologies,* edited by Gerald H. Anderson and Thomas F. Stransky, 128–131. New York: Paulist Press.
———. 1976b. *The Image of God among the Sotho-Tswana.* Rotterdam: A. A. Balkema.
———. 1979. "Where Are We in African Theology?" In *African Theology en Route,* edited by Kofi Appiah-Kubi and Sergio Torres, 59–65. Maryknoll, N.Y.: Orbis Books.
Shorter, Aylward. 1972. *African Prayers in Traditional Religion.* Maryknoll, N.Y.: Orbis Books.
———. 1974. *African Culture and the Christian Church: An Introduction to Social and Pastoral Anthropology.* Maryknoll, N.Y.: Orbis Books.
———. 1977. *African Christian Theology: Adaptation or Incarnation?* Maryknoll, N.Y.: Orbis Books.
Shorter, Aylward, ed. 1978. *African Christian Spirituality.* Maryknoll, N.Y.: Orbis Books.
Sidhom, S. 1969. "The Theological Estimate of Man." In *Biblical Revelation and African Beliefs,* edited by K. A. Dickson and Paul Ellingworth. Maryknoll, N.Y.: Orbis Books.
Sithole, Ndabaningi. 1954. *African Nationalism.* Oxford: Oxford University Press.
Smith, Edwin. 1950. *African Ideas of God: A Symposium.* London: Edinburgh House Press.
Sölle, Dorothee. 1974. *Political Theology.* Philadelphia: Fortress Press.
Sundkler, Bengt G. M. 1960. *The Christian Ministry in Africa.* London: S.C.M. Press.
———. 1961. *Bantu Prophets in South Africa.* 2nd ed. Oxford: Oxford University Press.
Taylor, J. V. 1963 and 1959. *The Primal Vision.* London: S.C.M. Press (1963) and Paris: Presence Africaine (1959).
Thomas, George B. 1977. "Kimbanguism: Authentically African, Authentically Christian." In *African Religions: A Symposium,* edited by N. S. Booth, Jr. New York: NOK.
Thomas, J. C. 1973. "What Is African Theology?" *The Ghana Bulletin of Theology* (Legon, June).
Thompson, G. 1975. "The Moratorium Debate." *International Review of Missions* 75, no. 254 (April).

Torres, Sergio. 1983. "The Irruption of the Third World: A Challenge to Theology." In *Irruption of the Third World: Challenge to Theology*, edited by Virginia Fabella, M.M., and Sergio Torres, 3–15. Maryknoll, N.Y.: Orbis Books.

Torres, Sergio, and John Eagleson, eds. 1976. *Theology in the Americas.* Maryknoll, N.Y.: Orbis Books.

Torres, Sergio, and Virginia Fabella, eds. 1978. *The Emergent Gospel: Theology from the Underside of History.* Maryknoll, N.Y.: Orbis Books.

Tutu, Desmond. 1974a. "African and Black Theologies: What They Mean." In *The Struggle Continues* (Third AACC Assembly at Lusaka).

———. 1974b. "Black Theology." *Frontier* 17 (Summer): 73–76.

———. 1975. "Black Theology/African Theology: Soul Mates or Antagonists?" *Journal of Religious Thought* 33 (Fall/Winter): 25–33.

———. 1979. "The Theology of Liberation in Africa." In *African Theology en Route,* edited by Kofi Appiah-Kubi and Sergio Torres, 162–168. Maryknoll, N.Y.: Orbis Books.

Van der Merwe, W. J. 1957. *The Shona Idea of God.* Fort Victoria: Morgenster Mission Press.

Wallerstein, Immanuel. 1961. *Africa: The Politics of Independence: An Interpretation of Modern History.* New York: Vintage Books.

———. 1972. *Africa: The Politics of Unity.* New York: Vintage Books.

Wambutda, Daniel N. 1980. "Hermeneutics and the Search for Theologia Africana." *Africa Theological Journal* 9, no. 2 (April): 29–39.

———. 1981. "Savannah Theology: A Biblical Reconsideration of the Concept of Salvation in the African Context." *Bulletin of African Theology* 3:137–153.

Wilmore, Gayraud, and James H. Cone, eds. 1979. *Black Theology: A Documentary History 1966–1979.* Maryknoll, N.Y.: Orbis Books.

Wilson, Monica. 1971. *Religion and the Transformation of Society: A Study in Social Change in Africa.* Cambridge: Cambridge University Press.

World Student Christian Federation. 1970. *A New Look at Christianity in Africa.* Vol. 2, no. 2. Geneva: WSCF Books.

Zvobgo, C. J. M. 1973. "The Influence of the Wesleyan Methodist Missions in Southern Rhodesia 1891–1923." In *Christianity South of the Zambezi,* edited by J. A. Dachs. Gwelo: Mambo Press.

Index

Compiled by William Schlau

8438